5/14

German Europe

For Elisabeth

German Europe

Ulrich Beck

Translated by Rodney Livingstone

polity

First published in German as *Deutsches Europa* © Suhrkamp Verlag Berlin 2012

This English edition © Polity Press, 2013
Reprinted in 2013

Polity Press
65 Bridge Street
Cambridge CB2 1UR, UK

Polity Press
350 Main Street
Malden, MA 02148, USA

ISBN-13: 978-0-7456-6539-9

A catalogue record for this book is available from the British Library.

Typeset in 11 on 14 pt Sabon
by Toppan Best-set Premedia Limited
Printed in the USA by Edwards Brothers Malloy

The publisher has used its best endeavours to ensure that the URLs for external websites referred to in this book are correct and active at the time of going to press. However, the publisher has no responsibility for the websites and can make no guarantee that a site will remain live or that the content is or will remain appropriate.

Every effort has been made to trace all copyright holders, but if any have been inadvertently overlooked the publisher will be pleased to include any necessary credits in any subsequent reprint or edition.

For further information on Polity, visit our website: www.politybooks.com

Contents

v

Contents

Preface

Will the Greeks have returned to the drachma or the Germans to the D-Mark by the time readers pick up this book? Or will they simply laugh the idea out of court because the crisis will have long since been overcome and Europe will have emerged from it strengthened? The fact that we even ask such questions and that we seem to be stumbling around in a fog of uncertainty tells us a lot about the elusive state of affairs in Europe and the risk involved in attempting to capture it in words.

Everyone knows what that risk is but to utter it is to violate a taboo. The fact is that Europe has become German. Nobody intended this to happen, but, in the light of the possible collapse of the euro, Germany has 'slipped' into the role of the decisive political power in Europe. Timothy Garton Ash summed up the situation in February 2012. 'In 1953 the novelist Thomas Mann appealed to an audience of students in Hamburg to strive for "not a German Europe but a European Germany". This stirring pledge was endlessly repeated at the time of German unification. Today we have a variation that few foresaw: a European Germany in a German Europe.'[1]

How could this come to pass? What might its consequences be? What threats does the future hold? What are its attractions? These are the questions I propose to address in this essay.

At the present time, public debate on the subject is dominated almost exclusively by its implications for the economy. There is an irony here when we recall how the crisis took the economists by surprise. The problem created by a purely economic analysis is that it overlooks the fact that the crisis is not purely a matter of the economy (and of thinking about the economy) but is also one of society and politics and our prevailing ways of thinking about them. It is not that I am venturing onto the alien terrain of economics but that economics has lost sight of the society it is analysing.

My intention in this essay is to put forward a new interpretation of the crisis. I should like to try to get to the bottom of the announcements in the daily press or on TV and to set them in a broader context. The reading I offer is based on my theory of the risk society. The vision of a modernity that has gone out of control as I have presented it in a number of books is one I shall develop further here with reference to the crisis of Europe and the euro.

There is a widespread view that what we need to overcome this crisis is more Europe. But we find less and less assent to the idea of 'more Europe' among the people of the member states. Given this situation, is it even possible to conceive of the completion of a European political union? Of a common taxation system and a common economic and social policy? Or is it not the reality that the preoccupation with a political union has obscured the crucial question, that of a European society, for so long that we have ended up leaving the most important factor out of the reckoning altogether? That factor is the sovereign people, the citizens of Europe. So let us put society back in. What needs to be done in the midst of this financial crisis is to shed light on the power shifts in Europe and to delineate the new landscape of power. That is the goal of this essay.

Ulrich Beck
August 2012

Acknowledgements

I dedicate this little book to Elisabeth, my beloved wife, also known as Professor Beck-Gernsheim, for discussing its intellectual architecture with me sentence by sentence, and for her unpretentious sensibility to the way that words and sentences have a life of their own. Without John Thompson, my great colleague and dear friend, this book would never have been written. His power of inspiration made me do it. Rodney Livingstone, who loves and lives German and English literature, gave his imagination as a present and reinvented my argument for the English-speaking world, lending it a classical note, the aesthetics of truth.

Nevertheless, all that is wrong or missing is, of course, my responsibility entirely.

Introduction

Europe: To Be or Not to Be:
The Decision Facing Germany

'Today the German Bundestag will decide the fate of Greece.' That was the announcement I heard on the radio at the end of February 2012. That was the day of decision on the second rescue package, which was tied to additional austerity measures as well as to the condition that Greece should accept a further loss of control over its own budget. 'Of course', I heard a voice in me saying, 'that's the way it is.' The other voice in me asked – incredulously – how was that possible? What does it mean for one democratic state to decide the destiny of another democratic state? I understand that the Greeks need German taxpayers' money, but the proposed cuts amount to an assault on the autonomy of the Greek nation.

What I found irritating at the time was not simply the substance of the announcement but also the fact that it was accepted in Germany as if it were the most natural thing in the world. Just listen to it again. The German parliament – not the Greek parliament – will decide the fate of Greece. How can that statement have any meaning at all?

Let us perform a small thought-experiment. Let's assume that the Germans were to hold a referendum on whether the Greeks should leave the euro now (i.e., the summer of 2012). The probable result would be 'Bye-bye, Acropolis'.[1] Let us assume further that the Greeks were to hold a referendum on the same question. The probable result would be a clear majority in favour of retaining the euro (with roughly 85 per cent in favour, according to opinion polls of May 2012).[2]

How are we to go about resolving disagreements between national democracies? Which democracy should prevail? By what right? With what democratic legitimation? Or is the coercive might of the economy to play the key role? Should the withholding of credit be the ultimate decisive factor? Or should Greece, the original home of democracy, be shorn of its right to democratic self-determination because of its debt burden? What sort of country, what sort of world, what sort of crisis are we living in, if we can stand by and watch one democracy emasculated by another without its provoking *any* feeling of outrage? More-over, the assertion that 'the German Bundestag will decide the fate of Greece' understates the situation. It is Europe that is at stake here. The statement 'Today it is Germany that will decide on the existence or non-existence of Europe' sums up the intellectual and political dilemma.

The European Union has twenty-seven member states, governments and parliaments; it has its own Parliament, a Commission, a Court, a High Representative for Foreign Affairs, a Commission President, a Council

President, etc., etc. But, thanks to its economic might, Germany has been catapulted by the financial crisis and the crisis of the euro into the position of the undisputed great power in Europe as a whole. After the Second World War and the Holocaust, Germany lay in ruins both morally and physically. Now, after barely seventy years, it has advanced from the status of eager pupil to that of schoolmaster of Europe. In the Germans' conception of themselves the word 'power' is still a dirty word, one that they like to replace with the word 'responsibility'. National interests are discreetly concealed behind such grandiose terms as 'Europe', 'peace', 'collaboration' or 'economic stability'. To utter the words 'a German Europe' is to break a taboo. To say that 'Germany will assume the "Führung" [leadership] of Europe' would be even more offensive.[3] We could say, however, that Germany assumes 'responsibility' for Europe.

But the European crisis is coming to a head, and Germany finds itself faced with a historic decision. It must attempt either to revive the vision of a political Europe in the teeth of every obstacle or to stick with a policy of muddling through and of using hesitation as a means of coercion – until the euro do us part. Germany has become too powerful to be able to afford the luxury of indecision.

The fact that the moment of decision is now upon us is rarely stated in so many words in the German media. But it is frequently referred to in the commentaries of foreign observers. Here for instance is the view of Eugenio Scalfari, the Italian journalist and writer: 'If Germany continues to pursue a financial policy that leads to a collapse of the euro, then the Germans would be responsible for the collapse of the European project. That would be its fourth crime after the two world wars and the Holocaust. Germany must now accept its responsibility for Europe.'[4]

No one should be in the least doubt. In a German Europe, Germany would be made to bear the responsibility for the failure of the euro and the EU.

I

How the Euro Crisis is both Tearing Europe Apart and Uniting It

**How German austerity policies are dividing Europe –
the governments are for it, the peoples are against**

In contrast to earlier empires, which traced their origins
back to myths and heroic victories, the European Union
was born out of the agony of war and as a response to
the horrors of the Holocaust. Today it is the financial
crisis and the crisis of the euro that has revealed to
Europeans that they do not live in Germany, France or
Italy, etc., but in Europe. And, to the extent that state
bankruptcy, economic crisis and the decline of the labour
market coincide with expectations heightened by the
expansion of education, the crisis generation is discovering that its fate too is European.

Almost one European in four under the age of twenty-
five is unemployed and many more are trying to survive
on short-term contracts. In Ireland and Italy around
one-third of those under twenty-five are jobless, according to official figures, while in Greece and Spain youth
unemployment was running at 53 per cent in June 2012.

In Great Britain youth unemployment has risen from 15 to 22 per cent since the onset of the credit crunch in 2008. In Tottenham, where the riots broke out in 2011, there are fifty-seven jobseekers for every vacancy.[1]

Wherever the new vulnerable educated class, the so-called precariat, erects its tents and raises its voice in protest, what it calls for is social justice – and its demands are put forward forcefully but also non-violently in Spain and Portugal, as well as in Tunisia, Egypt and Israel. The Facebook generation then carries this protest further, with the support of a majority of the population in the different countries. Europe and its youth are united in fury about a policy that spends unimaginable sums of money on rescuing banks while squandering the future of the young generation.

The crisis and the various programmes to save the euro reveal the contours of a different Europe, a divided continent, furrowed by new rift valleys and crisscrossed by new frontiers. One of these new rift valleys runs between the nations of the north and south, between creditor and debtor nations. Another runs between the members of the eurozone, who are compelled to take action, and the members of the EU who did not join the euro and who now have to look on without being consulted as key decisions are taken about the future of the union. A third rift has opened up during elections in the debtor nations, a rift that will have enduring political repercussions. This is the fact that governments vote for austerity measures, while peoples vote against them. What it reveals is the structural divide between a European project that has been devised and administered *from above*, by political and economic elites, and the resistance that wells up *from below*. Ordinary voters reject as highly unjust the demand that they should swallow medicine that may well prove lethal. Resistance is building not just in Athens but also throughout Europe as a whole to a policy aimed at overcoming the crisis by redistributing wealth *from bottom to top* in accordance with the principle of state socialism for the banks and the affluent, neo-liberalism for the middle classes and the poor. What will the rescuers do if the people they claim they want to rescue say they do not want to be rescued? At any rate, not by the methods proposed by their own governments, who tell them that there is no alternative?

It is a further paradox that we are experiencing an unprecedented wave of passionate debates and power struggles – only to find that we are all worse off in the end. The Germans are up in arms because 'German money [is being] thrown away on the bankrupt Greeks', as the inflammatory headline in the tabloid newspaper *Bild* expressed it. *Focus* magazine struck a similar note when it produced a now notorious cover picture showing the Venus de Milo holding up a finger to the world. Meanwhile, in the countries most harshly affected by the crisis, many people think they are losers because the austerity policy pursued jointly by Germany and Brussels deprives them of their means of livelihood – and also of their human dignity. Thus populist passions are aroused in the different member states, playing each off against the other, so that they fail to recognize that they are all jointly the victims of the financial crisis and of the inappropriate tools that are being used to deal with it.

The upshot is that in future Europe will contain many Europes. One of these is the Europe *from below*, the

Europe of ordinary citizens who may not even know (or want to know) that they are citizens of Europe. At the moment there is a catastrophic mood in Europe, a mood made up of a combination of insecurity, fear and outrage, a mood encapsulated in the phrase 'I can't understand what is going on.' Bank crisis and credit crisis. Europe in crisis and the euro in crisis. Every day it's something different – or is it just the same thing over and over? Everyone is perplexed and somehow at a loss. In a major piece on people's fears and confusion, the journalist Holger Gertz wrote in August 2011, 'You can demonstrate against war and nuclear energy; proposals for new railway stations or runways are touchingly comprehensible and almost invite demonstrations in protest.' But when it comes to the financial crisis, he adds, quoting a left-wing politician, 'What are you supposed to write on the poster? "Crisis, piss off"?'[2]

What are we to make of the fact that nobody understands what is happening? To find an answer to this question I should like to take up ideas I first formulated in *The Risk Society* and developed further in the *World Risk Society*. My interpretation there is that this spread of non-knowing is an essential component of a dynamic process which currently has Western societies in its grip.[3] In a certain sense the risk society is always a *'might'* society. Nuclear power stations whose intricate inner workings we do not fully understand *might* have an accident; the financial markets, which even the stock-market jugglers no longer seem to understand, *might* crash. This is the subjunctive as a permanent condition. We live in the constant expectation of catastrophes that might occur tomorrow. The catastrophic subjunctive erupts violently onto the scene in our institutions and our everyday lives. It is unpredictable; it is no respecter of constitutions and the rules governing democracies; it is full to bursting with an explosive growth of non-knowing and it washes all known landmarks away.

These diffuse threats also foster something like a community feeling. Let us take the euro crisis as an example. Whole societies are discovering that their standard of living has fallen dramatically as a result of the austerity programmes. Throughout Europe, an entire generation has to face the fact that they are no longer needed when the stock market indices shown daily on television suddenly plunge downwards. The consequences of the crisis do not stop at national frontiers; international financial link-ups have long since become far too powerful for that. So people have started to ask what it all means: is my German pension secure if Greece goes bankrupt? How can a state go bankrupt? What does it mean for me? Who would have imagined even a few years ago that the very banks which vehemently object to any state interference might now be calling for heavily indebted states to bail them out and that these same states would now shower them with astronomical sums? Today we can all imagine such things happening. But that doesn't mean that anyone understands it.[4]

As was shown in *Risk Society*, the expectation of global catastrophe reaches deep into the psyche of ordinary people; as such it constitutes one of the twenty-first century's great forms of mobilization. This kind of threat, whose effects are felt throughout the world, is what makes it possible for us to understand the often unwelcome interconnections between our own lives and the lives of people in other regions of the world.

The achievements of the European Union

Fifty-five years after the signing of the Rome Treaties, which brought the European Economic Community into being, its successor is making desperate efforts to prove to the world and to itself that it can withstand the severest test in its history. Of course, many of the current problems are not homemade but are the product of the financial crisis of 2008 and the following years, in the course of which bank managers were converted overnight into believers in the state and governments provided huge rescue packages. But, even if we make due allowance for all of this, the present situation still reminds us of the crucial mistake attending the birth of the euro. A common market with, in part, a common currency was established in an economic space the size of a continent and with a correspondingly large population. However, its founders failed to take the step to a full economic union, with the consequence that the economies of the euro states could not be coordinated effectively. The idea of 'reciprocal nationalism', according to which the duty of every state is to keep its own finances under control, may work when the economy is flourishing but will fail at times of crisis. At the same time, the events of summer 2012 show clearly how everything is interwoven with everything else: if one country goes bankrupt, it drags others down with it.

Amid all the controversy it is often forgotten that the EU, despite its flaws, has many magnificent achievements to its credit. The EU has succeeded in turning arch-enemies into good neighbours – a miracle in itself; its citizens enjoy political freedoms and a standard of living of which peoples living in other parts of the globe can only dream. Thanks to EU membership, former dictatorships in Spain, Portugal and Greece have been transformed into stable democracies. With twenty-seven states (twenty-eight following the accession of Croatia on 1 July 2013) and more than 500 million people, the EU has become the largest market and trading bloc in the world. Its social and economic model – capitalism tamed by the welfare state – may be going through a difficult period, but it still possesses the resources and the energies with which to respond to the financial crisis. People from sub-Saharan Africa or the Arab world continue to regard it as the Promised Land and are willing to set out for its shores at tremendous risk to themselves. The fact that Serbia and other nations of the former Yugoslavia are eager to join the Union likewise testifies to its continuing attractions as a haven of freedom and prosperity. And now, all this threatens to fall apart.

It is a paradox that the very success of the EU is one of the reasons for the lack of esteem in which it is held. Many of its achievements are so much taken for granted that they would probably only be noticed if they were to disappear. Just imagine what it would be like if passport controls were to be reintroduced at frontiers and airports, if food standards ceased to be reliable, if there were no freedom of speech and the press (freedoms that are being flouted in Hungary, as a result of which the country is attracting critical attention). Or consider how it would be if students could no longer find jobs in Avignon or Barcelona without surmounting complicated bureaucratic barriers and if people could no longer travel between Paris, Madrid and Rome without having to change money and pay attention to exchange rates.

Europe has now become second nature to us, and this may help to explain why people may be tempted to give it up so lightly.

We find ourselves at a difficult historical juncture, one in which we should remind ourselves once again of Gramsci's definition of a crisis. Crisis, Gramsci says, 'consists precisely in the fact that the old order is dying and the new cannot be born'.[5] But this transitional phase is fraught with confusion. That is our situation today: it is a caesura, an interregnum, a simultaneous collapse and a new beginning – and an uncertain end.[6] Perplexity, fear, not-knowing, frustration, restlessness, but also the craving for change – all this is characteristic of opaque situations in which people's expectations no longer match the institutional arrangements that are meant to satisfy them. However, all these symptoms may be signs of an impending change, as we see if we think about the Reformation, the French Revolution, or the collapse of the Eastern bloc. Discontent is always the product of specific demands, rooted in history. We Europeans inhabit societies that have declared liberty *and* equality for all to be among their fundamental principles. As a sociologist, I am not surprised that people in Spain or Greece should protest when faced by a system that produces unfairness and inequality to such a degree and forces the weakest to shoulder the costs that have been generated by a finance system which has run amok. Such discrepancies between expectation and reality always act as drivers of social mobilization, and the fact is that in recent months and years we have seen people in New York, London, Madrid or Athens going onto the streets – a point I shall return to at the end of this essay.

The blindness of economics

Armies of experts are waiting in the wings to help us find our bearings amid the not-knowing and the lack of transparency created quasi-automatically by modern risk societies. The economists who give us their responses to the crisis make the situation more easily comprehensible, but at the same time the 'interpreters of capitalism'[7] tend to reduce the complexity of the global financial markets in a disconcerting fashion. They personalize and emotionalize market events by introducing psychologically coloured terms into the essentially rational language of the stock exchange. They allege that 'nerves are raw' in the markets; that markets 'will not be fooled', are 'timid' or 'fearful' and inclined to 'panic reactions'.

We might also say that the economists' viewpoint is politically and socially blind, that it blinds others too and that the economic advice that dominates discussion is based on political and social 'illiteracy' (Wolfgang Münchau).[8] The general blindness may stem from the fact that the world's economists always base their opinions on some model or other and, if the models do not fit, you have a problem. Wolfgang Münchau has elegantly described this situation in the *Financial Times*:

Macroeconomists conveniently tend to confuse a monetary union, for which they have no model, with a loose fixed-exchange-rate system or a single-currency area, for which they do. A monetary union is a hard thing to grasp, because it is neither a state nor a loose arrangement in which everyone retains full sovereignty. . . . There is some wiggle room about entry, especially for countries that have opted out such as the UK and Denmark. There is no wiggle room about exit.[9]

This last point shows very clearly how expert economists lead both politicians and the public astray. The fact is that many people talk as if Greece's exit from the euro would itself be the solution. For in that event it is more or less implicitly stated that the Germans would cease to 'bleed' for the Greeks. However, such statements are misleading and false. There are at least four reasons for believing this. First, there is no provision for a member state's exit from the euro. It could be done, if at all, only at the wish of the country concerned. But the majority of Greeks wish to remain in the single currency.

Second, a Greek return to the drachma would trigger a debt haircut that would affect banks and businesses worldwide, primarily the German, French and American institutions that had previously invested in Greek government bonds because they were offered on such 'favourable' terms. This means of course that a Greek exit from the eurozone might unleash a repeat of the Lehman Brothers' collapse.

Third, if Greece did leave, it would of course cease to receive further assistance from the European bailout fund. However, as a member of the EU fallen on hard times, it would still be entitled to aid. (This explains, incidentally, why the UK is pleading so vehemently for the introduction of eurobonds and for Greece to remain in the eurozone. For otherwise Britain too would be liable for further payments.) Since it is in no one's interest for Greece to collapse into chaos and anarchy – let alone revert to a military dictatorship – the remaining members of the EU would be compelled to support it with sums that today are unimaginable and incalculable. The economists neither can nor will grasp the scale of the social costs that a relapse into nationalism and perhaps also xenophobia, violence and dictatorship would bring to the Greeks, but also to Europeans and the international community. It is for this reason that no one is really in a position to 'calculate' which would be the more costly course of action – for the Greeks to leave the euro or to stay in it.

Fourth, we ought rather to discuss whether Greece should leave the European Union as well as the euro. Such a step would have catastrophic consequences for Greece itself, because the country would then be cut off from resources essential to its own survival (such as the subsidies from the Common Agricultural Policy). To be sure, if Greece were to leave that would also have grave consequences for other EU member states, when we reflect that Greece (together with countries such as Spain, Italy and Portugal, among others) protects the frontiers of the union.

Thus the ultimate costs of Greece or other countries leaving the euro do not become visible in the economists' abstract models. Savers would lose the major part of their possessions; the state would face the threat of collapse, the middle classes poverty, the poor exclusion, and all Europeans would be left to grapple long-term with costly economic, social and political problems.

European domestic politics: the national concept of politics is outmoded

Some years ago I wrote in my book *The Reinvention of Politics*,

---

> The model of Western modernity . . . is antiquated and must be renegotiated and redesigned. . . . [What is needed is] not just rule-enforcing but rule-altering politics . . . not just power politics but political *design*, the art of politics. . . . More and more often we find ourselves in situations which the prevailing institutions and concepts of politics can neither grasp nor adequately respond to.[10]

The reference to outmoded rules and institutions is above all a reference to the rules and institutions of the nation-state. The fact that these are no longer appropriate to our current problems and challenges and that the rules have to be changed has become painfully obvious in the current euro crisis. The idea that taxpayers in Germany, Finland or the Netherlands could be held responsible for risks to the budgets of other euro nations or the debts of Spanish banks would have been inconceivable in the old world of nation-states. But even the rules on which transnational organizations such as the European Commission, the ECB and the IMF insist before releasing further loans seem to lag behind events, as the crisis dramatically gathers pace. And even the idea that a fiscal union would enable Germany and other creditor nations to guarantee the budgetary policies of other euro countries is still hostage to national ways of thinking. Here too the rules should really be amended so as to make way for a common European economic and financial system. If we cling to the old rules, as has been done, for example, by the objectors who have launched actions in the Federal Constitutional Court in Karlsruhe to block the introduction of the European Stabilization Mechanism (ESM) and the fiscal union on the grounds that they conflict with the Bundestag's fiscal sovereignty guaranteed in the constitution, it soon becomes clear that these old rules and procedures for dealing with current challenges are far too slow and cumbersome.

In other words, there are times when it is right to pursue day-to-day policies in accordance with the rules and there are other times that call for more ambitious policies involving rule changes. If we are to find appropriate solutions to the euro crisis – or indeed the threat of climate change and a financial capitalism out of control – we need politics on a larger scale. The idea that in an age of globalized risks we can act in accordance with the principle that 'we'll cope on our own' turns out to be a catastrophic illusion.

In these circumstances, the simple distinction between internal and external, domestic and foreign politics can no longer be sustained. The crisis in Europe is forcing us to see how the old frontiers have become increasingly blurred. Many commentators have been calling for a European domestic policy for years, if not decades. This policy should be given democratic legitimacy and should cater for EU-wide interests in such areas as social policy, education and the economy. Now, confronted by a crisis, we can see the emergence of something akin to a Europe-wide domestic policy, although in the event it has little in common with the option we have just outlined. In the member states the question of Europe has become a topic for internal politics. In spring 2012 this became a real factor in the presidential elections in France and the parliamentary elections in Greece. In May 2012 Alex Tsipras, the new star of Greek politics, toured the capital cities of the EU, Berlin and Paris, in order to impress Greek voters with images of his competence on the European stage. Angela Merkel has dressed up as the Iron Chancellor for the benefit of her German public so as to demonstrate that she would no longer let the Southern European nations get away with their lack of discipline. David Cameron's statements on Europe have been designed to appeal to the resentments of the British public and to garner applause from bankers in the City of London.

Thus 'European domestic policy' currently means that politicians take their lead not from any concern for the European commonwealth but from national elections, the media and specific economic interests. Political survival at home is always the top priority. And that end, so it is imagined, is more surely attained by a sceptical attitude and the defence of national interests than by declaring a commitment to the future of the European Union. To take any domestic risk on behalf of Europe is something that does not even enter the minds of most politicians.[11]

Even President Obama's Europe policy is driven to a significant degree by domestic considerations: 'A stable, growing European economy is in everybody's best interests, including America's, because Europe is our largest economic partner. . . . If a company is forced to cut back in Paris or Madrid, that might mean less business for workers in Pittsburgh or Milwaukee.'[12] Thus the crisis of the euro jeopardizes American businesses and banks and with them Obama's re-election chances. Fighting for a second period in office, the US president shows his concern about Europe. But Merkel, whose thoughts and actions are guided by domestic calculations, has remained obdurate (up to now). She is less afraid of

Barack Obama than of the German voters, as *Der Spiegel* concluded tersely.[13]

The opposite stance, where domestic politics are governed by supranational, European interests, is encountered less often. One recent instance occurred when Wolfgang Schäuble, the German finance minister, argued for higher wage settlements in Germany in order to support the euro. He may be said to have acted as the European minister for wages policy. 'It is acceptable for wages to rise faster here than in all other EU countries. Wage increases here help to dismantle imbalances within Europe.'[14]

The EU crisis is not a debt crisis

The financial crisis has opened up a rift in the EU between north and south. This rift has been deepened further by the growing influx of refugees and the associated costs. The fact is that people fleeing from persecution, civil war and chaos constitute a burden not on Europe as a whole but, for the most part, only on the customs and border agencies in Greece, Spain, Italy and Portugal – i.e., countries whose economies are already weakened. Current EU rules specify that the country in which refugees arrive is the country in which the asylum procedures should be initiated and completed. Although they receive balancing payments from the EU, the southern nations feel exposed and exploited. It is easy to understand therefore why Europe's financially weak border states should be increasingly prone to xenophobia and aggressive behaviour and that this should extend to outbreaks of open violence towards refugees.

This gives us some idea of what is at stake. Not only must we prevent the collapse of the euro; an even more pressing need is to prevent the collapse of European values – open-mindedness, freedom and tolerance. Anyone who thinks of the European crisis purely in economic terms may easily miss what is truly at stake. The true task is to create a Europe that is able to find answers to fundamental change and the great challenges of the day without lapsing into xenophobia and violence. On the surface the European crisis revolves around debts, budget deficits and problems of finance. But the deeper, more authentic question is how much solidarity can and should be achieved in Europe.

Whoever equates Europe with the euro has already given up on Europe. Europe is an alliance of former world cultures and great powers, which are bent on finding an escape route from their own warlike past. The arrogance displayed by northern Europeans in their dealings with the allegedly lazy, undisciplined southerners reveals an altogether brutal cultural ignorance and an obliviousness of history. Do we really need to remind ourselves that Greece is not just a debtor nation but also the cradle of European civilization, its guiding ideas and values? Have the Germans forgotten how deeply indebted their intellectual history is to Classical antiquity?[15]

Friedrich Nietzsche long ago contrasted a European consciousness with narrow-minded German nationalism. 'We [homeless ones] are not nearly "German" enough . . . to be able to take pleasure in the national scabies of the heart and blood-poisoning with which European peoples nowadays delimit and barricade themselves against one another. . . .' He vehemently attacked 'a system of politics which renders the German spirit barren by making it vain', contrasting it with a very different vision: 'We are, in a word – and let it be our word of honour! – *good Europeans*, the rich heirs of millennia of the European spirit, its over-endowed but also deeply obligated heirs.'[16]

Without its values of freedom and democracy, without its cultural traditions and dignity, Europe is nothing.

2

Europe's New Power Coordinates: The Path to a German Europe

Europe under threat and the crisis of politics

The geological faults laid bare by the crises in world politics have served to frustrate routine expectations and doom the trusted instruments of theory and politics to failure. In response we are seeing something akin to a flight reflex among intellectuals. This applies not least to sociologists, whose theories and empirical studies tend to inquire into the *reproduction* of the social and political order instead of its *transformation*.[1]

Needless to say, such studies do generally envisage an element of social change. Even so, through all the fluctuations that actually occur, social scientists tend to ask how the society and the politics based on the nation-state can continue to reproduce themselves notwithstanding all these changes.[2]

However, if we look at the decisive events and trends of recent decades – I have in mind here the Chernobyl disaster, the collapse of the Soviet Union, the terrorist attacks of 9/11 on the World Trade Center, climate change, the credit crunch and the crisis of the euro – we find they have two features in common. First, before they actually happened they were *inconceivable*; and, second, they are *global* both in themselves and in their consequences. They are literally world events and they enable us to perceive the increasingly dense network of interconnections between people's lives and actions and to realize that these interconnections can no longer be comprehended with the tools and categories appropriate to the nation-state. These events were not just inconceivable in practical terms within the paradigm of the nation-state and its reproduction, they fall completely outside the national framework and thus render it open to question. By contrast, the theory of the risk society consciously starts from the ways in which modernity brings itself into jeopardy and goes on to focus on the unravelling of the nation-state in the face of the catastrophes that threaten it and the resulting changes in our understanding of power, social inequality and politics. In connection with the European crisis we may propose three theses.

First, we are experiencing today an inflationary expansion in the number of imminent catastrophes and breakdowns. Admittedly, we must immediately enter a caveat and distinguish clearly between the *rhetoric* of catastrophe and the catastrophe itself. That is precisely the meaning of the concept of risk in the theory of the risk society. Talk about risks always refers to catastrophes that are still to come and that we have to anticipate and forestall in the present.[3] In the context of the euro crisis, this means that, while there are already dramatic instances of personal and social catastrophes (many Greeks can no longer afford stays in hospital or even visits to the doctor; around half of Spanish youth is

---

unemployed), we are still at the stage of risk as far as the key institutions of the euro and the European Union are concerned.[4] The real catastrophe looming over us is the possible collapse of the monetary union, since this would lead to a chain reaction that might well bring down the European Union as a whole and even drag the global economy into the abyss. Thus at this point we again discover the catastrophic subjunctive that forms the conceptual framework of this essay.

Many people confuse the *risk* society with the *catastrophe* society. An example of the latter would be something like a *Titanic* 'society'. Such a society is dominated by the motto 'too late', by a fated doom, the panic of desperation. This essay is concerned to show – to stay within the metaphor – that the cliff can still be avoided if we change direction. In this sense there is a certain affinity between the theory of the risk society and Ernst Bloch's principle of hope.

Second, like other major risks (think of nuclear energy or climate change) the European risk is uncontrollable in principle. We can neither calculate in advance nor control such a catastrophe with the available tools of prediction and prevention, uncertainty management or insurance. The particular nature of this risk from a historical point of view is that its uncontrollability is homemade – indeed, that it was the result of deliberate policy. A common currency was introduced without establishing institutions with which to monitor and coordinate the economic and financial policies of the individual member states.

Third, risk implies the message that it is high time for us to act! Drag people out of their routine, drag the politicians out of the 'constraints' that allegedly surround them. Risk is both the everyday insecurity that is no longer accepted and the catastrophe that has not yet occurred. Risk opens our eyes and also raises our hopes of a positive outcome. That is the paradox of the encouragement we derive from global risks. To that extent risk is always also a political category, since it liberates politics from existing rules and institutional shackles.

Because so much is at stake, options have appeared that until recently seemed entirely implausible and were put forward only by outsiders. 'Financial transaction tax', 'eurobonds', 'banking union', 'bank licences' – all these words, which make some people nod in agreement and others shake their heads, conceal mini-revolutions. A 'banking union', for example, involves a technocratic utopia in which national budgets, a sacred pillar of democracy, could be threatened by interventions from Brussels or Frankfurt. At the same time, a system of 'joint liability' is envisaged which would turn upside down everything that has been taken for granted hitherto – the idea, for example, that under no circumstances would the Germans be forced to let their money be used to pay for what is referred to as 'the profligacy of the southern nations, who have been living above their means'.

Once again we see that, where the expectation of catastrophe determines public perceptions, the foundations of politics and society are disturbed; the old institutions are no longer able to solve the problems and the rules can and must be changed. This creates scope for negotiation, for smaller and larger revolutions, and indeed for changes that had previously been inconceivable. And, even if many current theories assert that we have reached the end of politics,[5] we are discovering the exact opposite at present: an age in which new forms of politics are emerging.

The direction that will eventually be taken by the nation-state in its social and political organization is open in principle. At least two very different scenarios are conceivable. I would call them the *Hegelian* scenario and the *Carl Schmitt* scenario.

In the first, Hegelian version, national egoisms go on claiming to provide solutions to the crisis until the front wheels of the political carriage called Europe are actually hanging over the cliff edge. In that situation the glimpse of the abyss may well bring salutary forces into being if, at the last moment, the actors are able to recognize that to continue further on their own will inevitably lead to disaster. We might say that the injunction to 'cooperate or die' might well assert itself behind the backs of politicians acting egoistically on behalf of their own country. In this sense, Hegel's 'irony of reason' might well have a historical opportunity here.

Two questions stand at the centre of this scenario. In the age of global risks, how can nationally organized politics recover its ability to act? And how can transnational cooperation be achieved by democratic means?

The Carl Schmitt scenario is significantly bleaker. As I have argued above, the expectation of catastrophe sets the political landscape in motion, opening up a power-play. New options appear on the table; risks can be exploited in order to gain power. This is the meeting point of the theory of risk society and Carl Schmitt's reflections on states of emergency. 'The exception is more interesting than the rule', Schmitt says. 'The rule proves nothing; the exception proves everything: it confirms not only the rule but also its existence, which derives only from the exception. In the exception the power of real life breaks through the crust of a mechanism that has become torpid by repetition.'[6] In the exceptional situation, i.e., 'the case of extreme need', of 'a threat to the existence of the state or something of the sort',[7] the existing order of things may legitimately be suspended in order to defend the common good. 'He is sovereign who definitely decides whether this abnormal situation actually exists.'[8] It must be pointed out that, whereas Schmitt focuses on the logic of the threat of war, the theory of the risk society focuses on the logic of risk.

The risk society is a (latent) revolutionary society in which the normal situation and the exceptional situation can no longer be clearly distinguished. In dealing with the threat to the euro and the European Union, the relevant players are effectively negotiating about an exceptional situation whose ramifications are no longer confined to individual nation-states. Instead we are facing a 'transnational emergency' which can be exploited in various ways (legitimated by either democratic or technocratic means) by a variety of players, including national politicians, the unelected representatives of European institutions such as the ECB, social movements, or even the managers of powerful financial organizations.

We should not think of these scenarios as mutually exclusive. The current political debates combine elements of both scenarios. Will technocrats from different countries join forces in their efforts to resolve the crisis and bypass national and European parliaments? Will populist politicians in individual debtor countries attempt to acquire 'democratic' mandates which will enable them to respond to the demands for austerity measures by exiting from the euro? Is there any way of convincing the citizens of Europe as a whole of the need to cooperate to reach a resolution of the crisis?

In all these questions one fact emerges with increasing clarity. This is the tension between the logic of risk and the logic of democracy. The fact that the concept of 'Europe' has become more or less synonymous with that of 'democracy' tells us something of the progress that the EU represents, as contrasted with the imperial, colonial and nationalist history of Europe. As against this, under the spell of global risk, we witness the growth of a compulsion to act speedily, in a way that threatens to bypass the rules of democracy. We can see from this that the rhetoric of threats is always also an empowering rhetoric. Hence the rhetoric of the imminent collapse of Europe may easily result in the birth of a political monster. This forces us to face up to the question: how much democracy will the impending catastrophe still permit?

Let us recapitulate the argument thus far. The European Union can develop in two directions. In the best case it will succeed in overcoming the belligerent tradition of the nation-states and master the current crises through democratic means. In the alternative scenario, technocratic reactions to the crisis will spell the end of democracy. What are alleged to be necessary measures will be justified by reference to the impending catastrophe, and all opposition will be declared illegitimate, with the consequence that absolutist government will become the norm.

At present it is not really possible to predict the direction that will be taken by the European Union in its efforts to overcome the crisis. There seem to be four causes of tension at this point. They are located in different dimensions and each is characterized by a pair of opposing concepts: (1) more Europe versus more nation-state; (2) action to avert danger versus action forbidden by law; (3) threats emanating from the logic of war versus threats emanating from the logic of risk; and (4) global capitalism versus national politics. I shall attempt to explore these four dimensions in greater depth.

More Europe versus more nation-state
The increasingly tangible risk of collapse has also produced the dream of a new Europe (a key proposition of risk theory). I would like to use the term 'Europe builders' to describe people who are fighting for a new Europe and who are developing new ideas for European reform and expansion. One of the new promising expressions they have put into circulation is that of a 'banking union'. It is with such terms that the Europe builders hope to shape the future of political union. Their key idea is based on the assumption that the cataclysm carries within it a cosmopolitan imperative: cooperate, introduce supranational rules, and change the existing political order.

The architects of a banking union have to contend with the problem that banks live transnationally, but die nationally. This suggests its own solution: overcome the national death of banks by bringing in transnational regulations. A new European authority will have to be established for this purpose. There is some suggestion that a kind of Europe-wide ministry of finance might be needed.[9] Such ideas provoke furious objections on the part of the 'defenders of nation-state orthodoxy' who regard it as sacrosanct. In defence of their position they insist – not without justification (we are talking about a contradiction after all) – that a democratic mandate is indispensable. Severin Weiland has commented on this question in *Spiegel online*:

> It is only to be expected that there will be massive opposition from national parliaments on this score. After all, it represents a frontal onslaught on their supreme prerogative: budgetary control. An over-powerful finance ministry would threaten the ultimate nightmare: a return to a quasi-absolutist rule, this time in the shape of the euro-finance ministers in Brussels. Referendums would be unavoidable in many member states, probably including Germany, under Article 146 of the Basic Law.[10]

A risk that threatens the very existence of the European Union calls for political initiative transcending the nation-state. The problem is that this insight and the nation-state system of politics do not fit together. It seems to follow that what used to be called 'revolution' now becomes part of the daily grind of politics. A head of government today is forced to hint at the overthrow of national politics out loud or else *sotto voce*; he or she has to take larger or smaller steps towards that end and perhaps even initiate such a policy and ensure that it prevails. Chancellors, prime ministers and presidents may be said to have to become 'part-time revolutionaries'.

In the course of these debates, demands for solidarity, democracy and justice turn up everywhere and threaten to 'explode the system'. Isn't there something missing from the ground plan of the new Europe – an additional 'democratic pillar'? Would it make sense to legislate for a European presidency and rule that the incumbent should be chosen by all Europeans in a direct Europe-wide election?

The orthodox believers in the nation-state resist all such revolutionary proposals on the part of the Europe builders. They turn the vision of 'more Europe' on its head, take up arms in defence of the nation-state and insist on the legal validity of the existing system. However, this puts them in the awkward position of blocking essential reforms and means that, in the eyes of the Europe builders, they become a part of the problem.

We can see that the breach with the existing social and political order is what happens when our daily problems become European while the institutionalized solutions continue to be framed in national terms. If member states were to cede control of their banks to Europe, they would not lose the ability to shape their own destiny but in the final analysis would gain increased independence in an age of which we can say with certainty that the global finance sector can no longer be regulated by national authorities alone.

The battle for a European banking union repeats the political drama that has been enacted time and time again in connection with climate change or following the terrorist attacks on the World Trade Center on 11 September 2001. Many things would be a lot simpler if only people, interest groups and politicians were to abandon the antiquated notion of national sovereignty and realize that sovereignty can only be regained on a Europe-wide basis – through cooperation, consultation and negotiation.

Action to avert danger versus action forbidden by law
Chancellor Merkel's Europe policy 'ignores and insults the Federal Constitutional Court'. That is the thrust of Heribert Prantl's critique in the *Süddeutsche Zeitung*:[11]

The Federal Constitutional Court can say what it wants; it can advise, request, demand and plead – the Federal Government does as it pleases and the Bundestag puts up with it. Once again treaties with simply unimaginable implications are passed in a few days, and even hours. The package of laws on the Fiscal Compact and the European Stability Mechanism (ESM) is to be forced through the Bundestag and the Bundesrat at the double.

Prantl accuses the executive of a 'regrettably short-sighted amateurishness':

The new treaties deal in vast sums, billions; they contain legal constructs hitherto unknown to the law. An ESM entity will be set up that will be above the law, an entity that can sue but cannot itself be sued, and can do whatever it pleases.

To forestall misunderstandings, it should be noted that Heribert Prantl too fears for the future of the European Union. What he has written, however, is typical of the arguments advanced by orthodox believers in the nation-state. He complains about things being done despite their being *forbidden* by the Basic Law without seriously asking whether such things ought rather to be *required* in order to save the euro, the European Union and, ultimately, the global economy from collapse. 'How much time pressure can the law put up with?' That is the question put in this context by Winfried Hassemer, the former vice-president of the Federal Constitutional Court.[12] By the same token, however, we must also be allowed to ask: how much delay can Europe put up with?[13] Whoever ignores or trivializes the danger threatening Europe in order to preserve the present constitutional arrangements in stone makes it too easy for himself.

Thus the Europe builders are in a difficult position. Their battle for more Europe is an appropriate response to the danger, but it is frequently ruled out by existing law. On the one hand, they are attracted by a federal model in which national parliaments transfer budgetary control to a central European authority and a strict ban on new debt is made mandatory for all member states. On the other hand, however, this leaves unanswered the question of how to *legitimize* such a transformation of nation-states into a European social, political and legal system. By appealing to the need to avert the present danger? Or by obtaining the formal democratic approval of national parliaments, even though the vast size of the necessary credits, the complexity of the challenges and the time pressure involved would make a rejection by national parliaments almost unthinkable and would leave room for no more than democratic quibbles about the small print?

The risk to the euro is endemic throughout the political system. For example, it is forcing the European Central Bank and especially its president, Mario Draghi, to mount rescue operations which derive their legitimacy from the need to avert the current dangers despite the fact that they can no longer be justified on the basis of the ECB's existing mandate. 'Collectively, we have to specify a path for the euro', Draghi said at the beginning of May 2012. 'If we want to have a fiscal union, we have to accept the transfer of fiscal sovereignty from national governments to a European organization. How is this to be achieved?'[14] At the end of July he even announced that he would do whatever it takes to preserve the single currency, and in 'whatever it takes', he evidently included methods that implied a complete break with the ECB's previous remit, which had been largely confined to combating inflation.

Thus the threat to the euro has uncovered a novel, autonomous source of legitimation of a form of political action that aims at the *political transformation* of society and politics as found hitherto in the nation-state. The conflict between supporters of nation-state orthodoxy, who wish to keep politics within the existing rules, and the Europe builders, who advocate rule changes, is fed by the clash between actions that are 'illegitimate but legal' and those that are 'illegal but legitimate' and whose legitimacy is derived from the urgent need to ward off imminent dangers. This emergency politics is illegal to the extent to which it undermines existing nation-state democracy. The impending catastrophe empowers and even forces the Europe builders to exploit legal loopholes so as to open the door to changes that are in fact ruled out by national constitutions or European treaties.

This seizure of power under the banner of 'if the euro fails, Europe will fall apart' shocks some observers. Udo Di Fabio, a former Constitutional Court judge, regards it as a 'skewed pragmatism' that seeks to loosen or shrug off the legal constraints on politics. If we uncouple politics from the law, he warns, we shall lose an important landmark by which to orientate our political actions. 'If we dissolve the bonds between the state, justice and reason, we shall lose our compass for the humane and intelligent organization of the twenty-first century.'[15] Di Fabio overlooks the fact that the orthodox adherents of the nation-state have moved into the grey area of illegitimate legality because, while they have national – i.e., constitutional – right on their side, they have no answer to the threats facing Europe.

Threats emanating from the logic of war versus threats emanating from the logic of risk

What is meant by 'the transformation of politics' can also be seen in the transition from the threats emanating from the logic of war to those arising from the logic of risk. In the case of war, what we find is rearmament, resistance to enemies or their subjugation; in the case of risk we see cross-border cooperation to avert catastrophe – in other words, what I have referred to above as the Hegelian scenario.

In this context Carl Schmitt conducts his argument in terms of a binary us/them opposition. When he speaks of risks he always has opponents in mind. There is no room in this logic for the idea that mankind might jointly commit itself to pursuing a particular goal, or that something like cross-border cooperation could exist for any purpose other than combating an external enemy. Schmitt writes: 'The concept of humanity is an especially useful ideological instrument of imperialist expansion, and in its ethical-humanitarian form it is a specific vehicle of economic imperialism. Here one is reminded of a somewhat modified expression of Proudhon's: whoever invokes humanity wants to cheat.'[16]

Thus life and survival within the horizon of global risk follow a logic that is diametrically opposed to this. In this situation it is rational to overcome the us/them opposition and to acknowledge the other as a partner and democratic fellow player, instead of treating him as an enemy to be destroyed. The logic of risk directs its gaze at the explosion of plurality in the world, which the friend/enemy gaze denies. The world risk society opens up a moral space that might (though by no means necessarily will) give birth to a civil culture of responsibility that transcends frontiers and antagonisms. The two sides of global risk are, on the one hand, the traumatic experience of the vulnerability of all and, on the other, the resulting responsibility for all, including one's own survival. Looked at in this way, reminding ourselves of the ways in which the human race jeopardizes its own existence has connotations of an egotistical realism: whoever speaks of mankind wishes to save himself.

A further distinction between the two logics of the threats facing us is as follows. The military enemy with whom one engages is clearly identifiable; he has a name. We generally possess the information we need about his aims, his equipment and the strength of his forces. By contrast, when we come to the logic of risk there is often no clearly identifiable actor and no hostile intention. The threat is not direct, intentional and certain, but indirect, non-intentional and uncertain. We are speaking here of global risks that have come into the world in times of peace as the uncontrollable side-effects of the desired development towards more market, more consumption, more tourism, more technology, more transport – in short, as the side-effects of the victory of modernity.

To forestall any misunderstandings we must remind ourselves that the ancient paradigm of war is by no means obsolete even today. Even the most cursory glance at current or imminent conflicts makes this more than clear. (Think of the civil war in Syria or the simmering tensions between Israel and Iran.) However, in a globalized modernity it is the threats posed by risk that set our lives and power relations in motion. We know that wars result in inconceivable destruction and suffering to humanity. But what we are only beginning to suspect is how, in the midst of peace, risks can turn into cataclysms that overwhelm whole countries and even continents, robbing countless masses of their livelihoods. Quite without the use of tanks, helicopters and bombers, merely through the power of risk alone, an achievement such as the European Union together with all its institutions can be brought to the verge of collapse.

A nation's consciousness is shaped and renewed through confrontation with the enemy. This becomes second nature. In the case of risk the opposite logic applies. What counts here is not differentiating and arming oneself, not barricading oneself behind images of the enemy and high-tech weapons systems, but cross-border communication and cooperation, the inclusion of national, religious, etc., others, the willingness to meet other people halfway – these are the things that now become mandatory parts of the historical rationality of action. It is no exaggeration to say that overcoming images of the enemy becomes the national *raison d'état*.

In the world risk society a paradox has become evident. Where we are threatened with immolation the fate of other countries and regions cannot leave us unconcerned. The crisis has not just torn Europe apart; it has also brought Europeans closer to one another. Plenty of people have now begun to study the problems of the Greek economy with greater zeal than those of the labour market in their own backyard. How often have we been told that Europe lacks a proper media presence – and now? Never before have people talked so much about Europe. It is to be found on the front pages of the daily newspapers, in the business section, the culture section, the local news, in the village and at the dinner table. Will the prospect of the demise of the European Union end up promoting a European consciousness, a consciousness that takes issue with both the abstract Brussels-dominated Europe and with nation-state orthodoxy?

Global capitalism versus national politics

In the wake of the collapse of Soviet communism, capitalism has become globalized and, as the general consensus would have it, has largely spun out of the control of political leaders. Whether conservative, social-democrat or green, politicians of all parties feel they have become pawns in a power game orchestrated by global capital. 'No one can make politics that runs counter to the markets.' This dictum of Joschka Fischer's has been paradigmatic for the way the political class has regarded itself in the last two decades.

In view of the impending catastrophe, national governments and the representatives of Brussels institutions find themselves compelled to take action. Whoever fails to act – or 'merely' pretends to do so – is committing political suicide. The present risk imposes a search for alternatives and new options. By way of response, a 'revolutionary cell' of Europe builders has been formed, consisting of José Manuel Barroso, Commission President; Herman Van Rompuy, President of the European Council; Jean-Claude Juncker, President of the Euro Group; and Mario Draghi, President of the European Central Bank. They have advanced proposals for a banking union, a banking licence for the European bailout scheme, the introduction of a financial transaction tax, and the separation of investment banking and retail banking, and are considering the establishment of a European finance minister who would have a key role in reining in a finance capitalism out of control.[17]

It was formerly believed that, since there are, and can be, no global political solutions to global risks, nothing could be done. The debate on the financial transaction tax shows that this legitimizing of inaction is now a thing of the past. In the meantime, even the conservative/neo-liberal government in Germany has come round to accepting the idea of such a tax and is even prepared to force it through in a 'coalition of the willing' – i.e., a cross-border and cross-party coalition – and against the resolute opposition in particular of the United States and Great Britain. It remains true nevertheless that the Europe builders face a massive obstacle in these and similar initiatives (such as eurobonds or the transfer of sovereign rights to Europe). They may indeed be secretly convinced that they have the correct solutions to the crisis, but they are very aware that such measures will be enormously unpopular in the various member states and could represent a threat to the re-election of national governments.

The new landscape of European power

The European Union speaks with many voices: those of the presidents of the Commission and the Council and of the High Representative, as well as of the heads of government who assume the chairmanship of the EU in rotation, and of course of the politicians in Paris, Berlin and London, etc. It used to be fashionable to deride this cacophony, but suddenly Europe has acquired a telephone. It is to be found in Berlin and belongs – at present – to Angela Merkel.

This is just one example of the thesis advanced above that risks can lead to massive tectonic shifts in the landscape of power. Before offering a sketch of the rifts that have opened up in the course of the crisis, I should like to start by describing two of last year's events to show in concrete terms how the microcosm of rules and institutions has changed.

In October 2011 the heads of all twenty-seven EU states met in Brussels to discuss the future of the community – an important topic without a doubt – but the problem that weighed most heavily on the minds of a majority of the participants was different: it was how to rescue the European currency. With the discussion having dragged on all afternoon, Van Rompuy, the President of the Council, found he had no alternative, and just before 8 p.m. he broke with a taboo. He ushered the ten heads of government of the non-eurozone countries out of the room, including such heavyweights as Britain's David Cameron and Poland's Donald Tusk. The remaining eurozone leaders could then proceed to 'the important item on the agenda and they went on to discuss how to save the euro'.[18] The loss of influence on the part of the EU members not in the eurozone could not have been demonstrated more vividly.

The second example: 'Free speech again – at long last' – this was the title of a report in the *Süddeutsche Zeitung* at the end of May 2012 on the EU summit at which the newly elected French president, François Hollande, took part in the discussions for the first time. While many politicians were secretly pleased to see the end of the

'Merkozy' double act following the electoral defeat of Nicolas Sarkozy, such reactions themselves speak eloquently about the changes in the European hierarchy in recent years. The numerous crisis sessions of the past months were dominated by Angela Merkel and her French colleague, who withdrew from meetings to hold exclusive consultations together. Other Europeans, those of the second class, were forced to wait for periods well beyond the limits of the bearable, after which they were simply presented with the solutions supplied by the two leaders. According to the EU correspondent of the *Süddeutsche Zeitung*, Luxembourg's prime minister, Jean-Claude Juncker, was said on one occasion to have canvassed colleagues with the proposal to respond to the absence of the duo by simply disappearing. Politicians from the smaller EU member states especially 'found it liberating to be able to speak their minds freely again following the departure of Sarkozy'.[19]

After the painful summit in October 2011, *Der Spiegel* arrived at this conclusion: 'This brought the contours of a new Europe into focus, and it will be a divided Europe. The new frontier runs between the euro and the non-euro states.'[20] This observation is spot on, although the dividing lines are less clear-cut than this suggests. There are at least three dimensions to the new inequality in Europe: first, the division between eurozone nations and EU members; second, the split within the eurozone countries (creditor versus debtor nations); and, third, the creation of a two-speed Europe.

The division between eurozone nations and EU
As a former world power, Britain will be the greatest victim of the division between eurozone countries and

countries that are merely members of the EU. Britain is drifting into European irrelevance, but it cannot escape the implications of decisions negotiated and taken within the exclusive club of eurozone countries affected by the crisis. As far back as December 2011, David Cameron, a vehement Eurosceptic and representative of nation-state orthodoxy, vetoed the Fiscal Compact to achieve greater budgetary discipline. Since then the Conservative–Liberal coalition government in London has also rejected the proposed banking union. It insists on regulating banks according to its own ideas and wishes above all to prevent any action that might weaken London's position as a financial centre.

However, Britain's power of veto, which derives from its EU membership and which has enabled London to block further European developments hitherto, has suddenly lost its efficacy because the eurozone states are pressing on regardless. At the same time, Britain is, with France, the second-largest economy in the EU (in terms of purchasing power), but as such it is tied into the European economy for better or worse. About 55 per cent of British exports go to the EU. A break-up of the single currency would strike at the heart of the British economy. It is obvious, then, that British and European interests cannot be separated. In other words, the euro crisis can only increase Britain's need to retain its place at the negotiating table, but, as a member only of the EU and not of the eurozone, it has to leave the room when it really matters.

Strategically, an important consequence of this internal division is that the Eurosceptics and anti-Europeans are becoming isolated. The fact that a foundation stone, a dogma, of the EU (the sacred law of unanimity) has been undermined and partly replaced by qualified majority voting has the effect of increasing the weight of eurozone members. This new situation may lead some of the non-members of the eurozone (such as Poland) to consider joining the euro – despite the crisis, or even because of it.

The division between creditor and debtor nations
A dramatic gulf has opened up at the epicentre of the crisis-ridden states of the eurozone, in particular between those countries that are already (or not yet) on a drip provided by the rescue funds and those countries that are financing the bailout. The former have no alternative to accepting what I would like to call the authority of German euro-nationalism – that is, an extended European version of Deutschmark nationalism, which was the currency of German power. In this way the German culture of stability is being elevated to the guiding idea for Europe. At present, both Italy and Spain share the fate of being eurozone members and hence members of the new centre of power, but at the same time they find themselves disempowered. (Paradoxically, both countries are the home of intellectuals whose enthusiasm and commitment to the European idea have scarcely any equals elsewhere.)

From this perspective, the EU can be seen to possess two layers of outsiders. The outermost layer consists of countries belonging to the EU but that do not have the euro. The innermost layer of outsiders consists of those who have the euro but are dependent on the financial assistance of the other member states. These new debtor nations might be said to constitute the new 'underclass' of the EU. They are compelled to acquiesce in their loss of sovereignty and endure blows to their national pride. Furthermore, their democratic right to self-determination dwindles to the alternative: acceptance or exit.

The meaning of European cooperation and integration has become fundamentally ambiguous, and it is above all the new underclass that is suffering from this ambiguity. Its fate is uncertain: in the best case, it will be federalism, in the worst, neo-colonialism. If we so wish we can regard this as a backward step for democracy. In feudalism, only the aristocracy had a say. Are we witnessing the revival of such privileges? In our system of risk capitalism, do only rich nations have a choice, while the debtors have to content themselves with a mere shadow democracy, a quasi-democracy? The other side of the coin is that, because Germany is the wealthiest country, it has the only real say at the centre of Europe.

The creation of a two-speed Europe

The two divisions sketched above have called into existence a third – through the back door, as it were – namely, a two-speed Europe. The idea that groups of member states should be able to pursue a policy of integration in certain areas has been aired frequently since the 1980s. In a much discussed keynote speech on European politics in 2000, Joschka Fischer, the German foreign minister of the day, reflected on the idea of a 'centre of gravity' that would act as an avant garde, a 'locomotive', that would accelerate the process of political integration.[21] Such proposals have always been controversial because they run counter to the Union's idea of itself and the principle of unanimity, which had been sacrosanct for so many years. Fischer too has since retreated from this idea.[22]

Now the idea of a two-speed Europe has suddenly been revived, bypassing questions of its democratic legitimacy. The member states directly threatened by the crisis of the euro have overtaken the remaining EU nations and slipped willy-nilly into the role of Europe builders. This is a further example of the historical forces that have been unleashed by the anticipation of catastrophe.[23]

To sum up, it is easy to see that the three divisions outlined here all tend in the same direction. They all strengthen the leading position of Germany within the EU. At the same time, we can see that this increase in power is rooted in the dynamics of the political situation itself and may be said to have occurred 'behind the back' of the actors concerned and the public in general. In this sense, the growth in German power is a perfect illustration of the law of unintended consequences.[24] Writing on the same theme in the *Neue Zürcher Zeitung*, Eric Gujer claims: 'The majority of Germans would rather that their country were a greater Switzerland in a remote corner of world politics . . . Berlin is reluctant to act as leader, it does so at best in the economy, seldom in foreign politics and never militarily.'[25]

'Merkiavelli': hesitation as a means of coercion

Niccolò Machiavelli (1469–1527) was the first thinker to have identified a form of power that can be forged from the confusions of the age. He believed that profound crises that sow dissension and bring forth destructive conflicts are the driving force of history. Crises are invitations to the accumulation of power, but in certain circumstances they can also lead to its decline. This is the point at which Machiavelli's theory of power intersects with the theory of the world risk society. Impending catastrophes throw up opportunities (Machiavelli used the term *occasione*) that can be seized by a man – or indeed a woman – with a talent for power (*uomo virtuoso*). That is precisely what Angela Merkel has done. She has seized the opportunity that presented itself to her to restructure power relations in Europe. How she achieved this will be analysed at greater length in the following pages.

We must begin by noting that the confusion that reigns at present in the crisis of Europe and the euro is significantly greater than the muddle facing Machiavelli when he wrote his *Il Principe* at the turn of the sixteenth century. As we know, his cynically realistic guide to the expansion and maintenance of power was dedicated to a single prince, Lorenzo II de' Medici, the ruler of Florence. In the European Union, by contrast, there are many rulers, as befits its political architecture, and hence no one in overall command. After all, the EU is not a unified state with a single government, a parliament, a people and a constitution. It is based rather on an intentionally opaque set of power relations, in which European institutions exist in parallel and on a plane of equality with the governments, parliaments, etc., of the member states. It follows that the question of who possesses sovereignty can in principle never receive an unambiguous answer and that power has to be shared or renegotiated from one case to the next.[26]

The fundamental fuzziness of this dual existence on a national and a European plane is compounded by the additional opacity arising from the twofold crisis that has shaken the European Union to its foundations. Because of the weight of their debts, a number of individual member states are on the verge of bankruptcy. At the same time, these debts threaten the euro and, with it, the member states of the eurozone and ultimately also the EU. Whether or not all member states will be infected by the viral spread of the burden of debt, whether it calls for a joint response ('if the euro fails, Europe fails') or becomes the responsibility of the individual states, and, above all, who has the power to decide on behalf of everyone else – the consequence of the crisis is an increase in the self-destructive conflicts that, if anything, accelerate the threatened disintegration. The alarming novelty is not the fact that such fundamental conflicts have shaken the EU. The EU has always in principle functioned as an abbreviation for conflicts and crises. The fuzziness of the dual nature of EU sovereignty throws up such conflicts with the regularity of a metronome. What is new in the present situation is that the well-rehearsed strategies to avert, moderate or resolve such conflicts have ceased to function properly in the currency crisis and the negotiations about how to defuse it. This threatens to destroy the EU, and it defines the chaotic situation that leads to calls for a greater concentration of power.

Angela Merkel is widely regarded as the uncrowned queen of Europe. If we inquire into the basis of her power we become aware of one characteristic feature of her effectiveness: her tendency not to act at all, to decide the time is not yet ripe, to act at a later date – in short, to procrastinate. In the European crisis Merkel delayed taking decisions from the very outset. At first, she was reluctant to put the tragedy of Greek indebtedness onto

Hesitation as a means of coercion – that is Merkiavelli's method. This coercion is not the aggressive incursion of German money but the opposite. It is the threat of withdrawal, delay and the refusal of credit. If Germany withholds its consent, the ruin of the debtor nations is inevitable. Only one fate is worse than being overwhelmed by German money and that is *not* being overwhelmed by German money.[28]

This type of involuntary domination, legitimated as it is by a hymn to austerity, has been perfected by Angela Merkel. The European landscape of power is now being transformed by the epitome of unpolitical activity – i.e., doing nothing at all. By this means Germany's rise to the position of hegemonic power in Europe has been both advanced and concealed. That is the tactic of which Merkel is the master and which might indeed have come straight out of Machiavelli.

Thus the new German power in Europe is not based, as in former times, on force as the *ultima ratio*. It has no need of weapons to impose its will on other states. If only for this reason, all talk of the 'Fourth Reich' is absurd. Furthermore, power that is grounded in the economy is far more mobile. It has no need to invade and yet is ubiquitous. The pressure it can exert arises not from the logic of war but from the logic of risk – more exactly, that of the threat of imminent collapse. The strategy of denying assistance – *not* doing anything, not investing, making no credits and funds available – this much-used denial is Germany's key lever as an economic power in the Europe of financial risk.

Third, this is how Germany has succeeded in the seemingly impossible task of combining national electability and its role as Europe builder. But that also means that all measures designed to save the euro and the European Union must begin by passing the test of proving their suitability for domestic politics – i.e., of satisfying the question whether they will promote German interests and Merkel's own position. The more critical of Europe the Germans become, the more they feel beleaguered by debtor nations who want nothing better than to make free with the money in German pockets, the harder it will become to disentangle the mess. Merkiavelli has now responded to this problem by producing her trump card – the idea of a German Europe. Domestically, the Chancellor soothes the Germans who are in a rising panic about their pensions, their houses and their economic miracle by donning a mien of Protestant severity and administering doses of 'Noes' at regular intervals. By adopting such a policy she has advanced to the position of Europe's schoolmistress. At the same time, in foreign affairs she adopts a stance of 'European responsibility' by obtaining the support of the eurozone nations through a policy of the lesser evil. Her siren call is: better a German euro than no euro at all.

In this sense too Merkel has proved to be an astute disciple of Machiavelli. Is it better to be 'loved or feared?' he had inquired in *The Prince*. His answer is that 'one ought to be both feared and loved, but as it is difficult for the two to go together, it is much safer to be feared than loved, if one of the two has to be wanting'.[29] Angela Merkel may be said to apply this principle selectively. Abroad she is to be feared, at home she should be loved – perhaps because she has taught foreign countries to fear. Brutal neo-liberalism to the outside world, consensus with a social-democratic tinge at home – that is the successful formula which has enabled Merkel consistently to expand her own position of power and that of Germany as well.[30]

Fourth, Merkel wants to prescribe what actions should be taken by Germany's partners and even stipulate that they should adopt what passes in Germany for the magic formula for politics and the economy. The German mantra runs: save, save in the interests of stability. The political reality is unmasked as the good housekeeping practices of the famous or notorious Swabian housewife. However, these tend to turn quickly into radical cuts in the resources available for pensions, education, research, infrastructure, etc. We are faced here with a hardnosed neo-liberalism that is now to be built into the European constitution in the shape of the Fiscal Compact – bypassing the (feeble) European public sphere in the process.[31]

These then are the four components of Merkiavellianism – the combination of nation-state orthodoxy and Europe building, the art of hesitation as a means of coercion, the primacy of national electability and, lastly, the German culture of stability. They mutually reinforce one another and constitute the core of the power at the heart of a German Europe. There is even a parallel for Machiavelli's *necessità*, the historical emergency to which the Prince must be able to respond. This is the idea of Germany as what Thomas Schmid calls the 'good *hegemon*', who finds himself compelled to put the need to deal with imminent danger above the fact that certain actions are forbidden by law. In order to extend German austerity policies throughout Europe as a whole, democratic norms may have to be relaxed or subverted according to Merkiavelli. A series of consequences and questions flow from this.

The power hierarchy that is emerging in this way in the relations between democratic nations has in itself no democratic legitimacy but is a function of their different positions in world markets. The decisions taken here do not require legitimation to the same degree. They do not arise on the basis of democratic elections but are the product of economic power. They do not require foreign approval, but domestic approval is essential. To refuse to give German money to Southern European debtor nations is entirely legitimate and politically opportune in Germany.

But how can the German government's poker-faced 'Yes and No' on support for the euro and rescuing the EU possibly end up as a gain in power for the Germans in Europe? From the standpoint of the Europe builders, the governing principle is that strengthening the political union would create greater opportunities for all member states – and for them alone. They obtain a voice in impending decisions and can directly influence the course of European politics. At the same time, they can count on the support of the combined power of the EU in helping them deal with problems in their own country – whether in the realm of crime, natural disasters, a crisis in agriculture or the threat of national bankruptcy.

It is true, however, that in the course of the euro crisis the positive gains resulting from cooperation have turned into zero-sum games, and some players are registering massive losses. It appears that cooperation can take two very different forms. It can be based on mutual recognition or on hierarchical dependency. It is not unknown for a state to appeal for cooperation so as to conceal its own interests in control and domination behind the offer of recognition.

Put bluntly, at the moment it looks as if only wealthy and already powerful states can bank on cooperation as a way of gaining an increase in political influence, while the debtor states must fear that they will have to defer to the diktat of better-off 'European partners' and the rules they lay down. As soon as large as well as small states fall into the debt trap, the power of Germany with its Yes-and-No policy will make even further gains in Europe.

At the same time, we perceive once again that Germany's rise to the position of the leading power in 'the German Europe' is not the consequence of a secret master plan, cunningly conceived and adroitly executed. At least to begin with, it was the involuntary and unplanned product of the financial crisis and its anticipation of disaster. As matters progressed, we may suspect from the way in which they developed that a more conscious element of planning did enter into it. The Chancellor saw the crisis as her *occasione*, 'the propitious moment'. A combination of *fortuna* and Merkiavellian *virtù* enabled her to seize the historic opportunity and to profit from it both domestically and in foreign relations. Admittedly, something of an internal opposition is building, consisting of those who take the view that the rapid process of Europeanization disregards the rights of the German parliament and is therefore incompatible with the Basic Law. But Merkel has cleverly managed to turn even these bastions of resistance to her own advantage by integrating them into her policy of taming the opposition by means of her delaying tactics. Once again she is doubly successful; she has achieved more power in Europe and greater popularity at home, enjoying the favour of the German voter.

The Merkiavelli method may well gradually reach its own limits. After all, the German policy of austerity has yet to show any successes – quite the contrary, in fact. The debt crisis now threatens to engulf Spain, Italy and perhaps even France. The poor are becoming even poorer, the middle classes are threatened with decline, and up to now there has been no light at the end of the tunnel. In this case too, then, power may well lead to the formation of a countervailing force, especially now that, with Nicolas Sarkozy's departure, Angela Merkel has lost an important ally. The arrival of his successor, François Hollande, has brought a noticeable shift in the balance of power. Representatives of the debtor nations have been able to convene meetings with the Europe builders in Brussels and Frankfurt in order to find an alternative to the frequently populist austerity policies of Angela Merkel (and also Philipp Rösler, the Free Democrat minister of economics and technology), which are so clearly aimed at the German electorate with its ingrained fear of inflation. These meetings are designed to rethink the function of the ECB and persuade it to direct its efforts towards a policy of growth along the lines of the stance adopted by the US Federal Reserve.[32]

An entirely different scenario cannot be ruled out. If matters come to a head, Angela Merkiavelli, the hesitant European, could overturn her coalition with the Eurosceptic FDP and form a transitional government with the SPD in order to emerge as Europe's saviour and go into the elections in 2013 strengthened both domestically and on the foreign-policy front. In favour of this view is the reflection that Merkel has absolutely no interest in going down in the history books as the chancellor who presided over the demise of the euro.

From the burden of history to the burden of the schoolmaster

While other countries sink ever deeper into debt, the German economy continues to thrive, for the time being at least. That is reflected in the general mood in the country today. In politics, the media and among the public more generally, a new national pride has become evident, based on people's knowledge of their own achievements. This new attitude could be summed up in the words: we are not the masters of Europe, but we are its schoolmasters. This nationalism, with its swaggering gestures of 'We're somebody again!' and 'We know what's what', has its roots in what we might call 'German universalism'. Not only is Europe on its way to becoming German; the truth – that is, the truth of austerity politics – is on its way to becoming German as well. And the two things are linked.

What is the meaning of, first, German universalism and, second, of that same universalism when extended into European politics? Universalism is what occurs when I assert that I am in possession of criteria that enable me to decide questions of good and evil, right and wrong, and not merely here at home, but also there, among you, not just now but also tomorrow and in the future. This universalism cultivates a habit of mind that enables it to obliterate the stain of its origins in its

history at the centre of Europe. It achieves this by con-
ceiving of the world within the horizon of 'reason'. In
concrete terms this means it enacts a monologue, a
soliloquy, in seeking out the transcendental conditions
entailed in thinking about 'the world, you, God, other
people, history and the economy, and so on'. What is
neglected is the ability to see oneself through other's
people's eyes.

When extended to apply to European politics, this
universalism reveals that Germany's today is Europe's
tomorrow. Our own social experience and political
values are turned into absolutes. We forget or repress
or are blind to the fact that these values have limited
validity. Instead, we boldly assert that what's good for
the German economy is right for the European economy
as a whole, and beyond!

Many of our European neighbours do in fact contem-
plate the 'German jobs miracle' of full employment with
astonishment, admiration and even envy. Only a few
years ago Germany was the sick man of Europe, with a
stagnating economy and up to 5 million unemployed.
Now it is the champion, with growth rates of 3.7 per
cent and 3 per cent respectively over the last two years,
rates double that of the EU average. Joblessness has
almost halved and youth unemployment is down to a
third of its peak. Both at home and abroad, significant
sections of the economic, political, academic and media
elites recommend this achievement as a patent recipe for
Europe as a whole. It is confidently asserted that, if you
want to learn about the right policies to adopt in a crisis,
you need look no further than the German 'Agenda
2010'. This was the document in which the SPD/B'90/
Green coalition government under Gerhard Schröder,

the federal chancellor of the day, set out its principles for labour market reform.

The reforms announced in this document brought about a paradigm shift in the German labour market of 2002–3. The slogan it proclaimed at the time was 'Demand and Support', but its aim was to increase the pressure on the unemployed to accept job offers below their qualifications, at lower wages and on inferior terms. Employers' costs were significantly decreased by reductions in employer contributions to pension and medical insurance. However, the expected quid pro quo of an increase in investments and the number of jobs did not materialize. Germany began to see the benefits of its aggressive export economy only with the recovery of the global economy after 2006 and then in the crisis years of 2008–9. And this success came partly at the expense of the weaker EU members hit by the crisis. The 'bitter medicine' of its austerity policies had one far-reaching consequence. It universalized the emergence of the 'precariat'.

Roughly half the new jobs which were created are precarious. They are made up of around 1 million agency jobs, 7.4 million so-called mini-jobs (paying €400 per month), and 3 million temporary positions, etc. This has led to deeper social divisiveness and a rapid increase in the earnings gap between the rich and the poor.

German notions of stability and the policy of cuts designed to preserve it require indebted countries to impose massive austerity programmes in the teeth of popular resistance. Hitherto these austerity programmes have only intensified the economic crisis in Europe, leading to the opposite of what was intended. This is because economic downturn leads to reduced tax receipts while ratcheting up the costs of unemployment. That in turn increases the government deficit and leads to demands for even greater cuts, which succeed only in intensifying the crisis. Here we have the vicious circle into which Germany's universal austerity policy has plunged Europe's debtor nations.

The German defence of this policy of asceticism might well have come directly from Martin Luther and the Protestant work ethic. 'Suffering purifies.' The road through Hell, the road through austerity, leads to the Heaven of economic recovery.

At the heart of this policy lies a No without a Yes: no eurobonds; no increase in the funds available for the European stabilization policy (currently capped at 500 billion); no direct payments to refinance the broken banking system, only payments to the relevant debtor nations, which are thus held responsible for the implementation of the austerity policies; no raising of new debt for investment programmes to stimulate the economy.

This enables us to take a fresh look at the meaning of Europe, the meaning of the two letters E and U for Germans at the beginning of the twenty-first century. We can put the question even more forcefully: why does Germany still need Europe? The answer used to be self-evident, but because of the crisis, and also because of the integration of the countries of Central and Eastern Europe following the collapse of the Berlin Wall, the conditions underpinning that reply have undergone a significant change.

The fact is that, following the Second World War, Germany's links to the rest of Europe had a genuine

---

political substance. Until well into the 1990s, Germany's political goals could be reached only through an explicit commitment to Europe. That holds good in particular for its policy of reunification. Reunification could realistically be achieved only by adopting a transnational, cosmopolitan policy. Given the facts of the Cold War between East and West, reunification was inconceivable at the national level – i.e., as the product of direct negotiations with the GDR. The only realistic approach to restoring German unity involved making a 'cosmopolitan detour' via Europe, to say nothing of Washington and Moscow, where the nuclear threat could be used as a tactic for making the 'Iron Curtain' more porous. Up to that point, identifying with Europe was clearly in the national interest: the more European the policy, the greater the likelihood of success as a nation. In other words, following the era of German militarism and the Holocaust, and right down to reunification with the GDR and beyond, '*Europe*' provided the answer to the questions Germans asked about themselves. 'Germany is our native land, Europe is our future.' That was the form of words adopted by Helmut Kohl, the federal chancellor, in his government programme of 1991–4. His goal was 'the political unity of Europe'. And, during the first session of the all-German Bundestag, Willy Brandt proclaimed: 'Germany and Europe belong together now and it is to be hoped they will remain together in the future.' This conviction was written into the revised version of Article 123 of the German Constitution and so has become an integral part of the *raison d'état* of a united Germany.

With their universalist approach to austerity measures, Germany's political, economic and media elites have begun to apply the 'truths' learned during reunification to a crisis-ridden Europe. In the process, the West Germans' know-it-all attitude and their imperialist sense of superiority to the East Germans have been brought to bear on the alleged 'mismanagement' of the debtor nations. In other words, the process of unification with the bankrupt GDR has been used as the template for German crisis management in Europe – with the crucial distinction that the word 'solidarity' has been expunged from the vocabulary of the European debate. The key error in Germany's austerity policies does not lie simply in its unilateral and national definition of the European public good but above all in its arrogant conviction that it has the right to determine the national interests of other European democracies. And not simply in relation to the crisis in the euro and in finance, but elsewhere too – from ecology to nuclear energy – Germans feel they are in a position of responsibility. They feel the countries surrounding them are full of slackers. The Italians and the Spanish, the Greeks and the Portuguese, may be our superiors in their *joie de vivre*. But their fecklessness! Their lack of seriousness! They really should learn the meaning of budgetary discipline, tax morality and a more caring attitude to nature. They have still to learn that, in the globalized world, clean balance sheets and a clean environment must have priority.

So what the southerners need is some extra coaching, a kind of re-education in matters concerning saving and responsibility. For the majority of Germans this conclusion follows inexorably from the figures, and this explains why it would be a crass misunderstanding to believe that what we are seeing is German arrogance or

German power lust. After all, the Germans want only to help make Greeks, Spaniards and Italians better able to cope with the world's markets. At present, the Germans regard this as their historic task. Where Helmut Kohl promised to create flourishing landscapes in the former East Germany, Angela Merkel wants to achieve the same thing for the whole of Europe.

The importance of this new sense of their identity may perhaps be explained by the fact that it liberates Germans from at least some of the burden of the 'never again' syndrome: never again a Holocaust, never again fascism, never again militarism. So the pedagogical impulse of Germans today can also be explained in terms of their history. After all, the idea of a shared Europe itself dates back to the period after the Second World War, after the great military and moral disaster. Moreover, we should remind ourselves that what inspired that vision in the first instance was not the question of common European interests, but the desire of Germany's neighbours to integrate Germany into a larger whole, to tame its aggressive impulses and in that way to prevent further bloodshed and a new wave of destruction. That was the motive driving the post-war generation to create a new Europe. The so-called German question was a question put by Germany's neighbours, her former enemies, but it was also a question Germans addressed to themselves. How far have we internalized the values of the West – capitalism, freedom and democracy? Europe was the answer to these questions.

In the meantime, the Germans have learned their lesson. They have become model democrats, model nuclear dropouts, model savers and model pacifists. They have had to take a long, sometimes difficult journey to achieve this goal. The ghosts of the past were not easily laid to rest; in fact, they sometimes came all too readily back to life. Even today the 'utterly normal everyday fascism' of the past has not yet been overcome, in Germany as in other countries. But there can be no doubt that Germany has changed. Measured by its own history, this is the best Germany we have ever had.

Against this background it is easy to understand why many Germans have a palpable yearning for normality. After decades in which they had publicly to confess their sins, after over half a century of declaring that 'Never again would there be any National Socialism', we can discern in the media, politics and the general public the emergence of a counter-movement; we hear the sigh of a new 'never again': never again should they have to appear as penitents. The Germans no longer wish to be thought of as racists and warmongers. They would prefer to become the schoolmasters and moral enlighteners of Europe.

If this diagnosis is accurate, why should it be politically objectionable to speak of a 'German Europe'? The likely response would be: the burden of the past is still too great. The phrase 'a German Europe' is contaminated by history and breaks a highly sensitive taboo because it articulates the new power relations.

A German Europe: hierarchy instead of equal participation

To repeat, the creation of the European Union has up to now had positive results in the main. The member states have profited from it because the loss of national autonomy has been compensated for by the expansion of transnational sovereignty. The combined power of the EU can better solve many national problems than the member states could solve on their own. That is the win–win game of Europeanization.

Today, however, given the power constellation of a German Europe, we can see that Europeanization can assume two opposed forms, two varieties of integration and cooperation: either participation on terms of equality (reciprocity) or hierarchical dependence (hegemony). We have to relate the distribution of power and risk in Europe to the scope for action on the part of large states and smaller ones, powerful states and poor states, states that give credit and states that take it, if we are to assess the dynamics and potential for conflict between countries and societies that threaten to split Europe apart.

What then does it mean to speak of 'a German Europe'? The alleged coercion implicit in the austerity programme prescribed by Germany has meant that equitable participation has been sidelined and replaced with increasing frequency by forms of hierarchical dependency. By linking credits to rigorous reforms and the corresponding control mechanisms, entire regions have been plunged into social decline and countless people have been deprived of their livelihoods, their dignity, their future – and, not least, their faith in Europe.

The immense loss of trust can be measured by the fury of ordinary citizens and the protests and demonstrations in Greece, Spain and Italy. We may also look beyond these images of despair and think of them as the starting point for an important insight. They enable us to identify four principles on which to build trust in Europe, the indispensable foundation of a European society.[33]

The principle of fairness The expansion of Europe also
  leads to new dependencies and obligations. What is
  crucial is that the methods adopted as well as the results
  achieved should be perceived as *fair* and *just* by all par-
  ticipating parties.

The principle of equalization The question of how the
  large, powerful members of the Union treat the smaller
  states will decide whether Europeans will get along
  together in the future – and indeed whether Europe can
  survive as an entity. Unilateral interventions by powerful
  states have to be prevented in the interests of trust and
  stability. There must be an element of equalization in the
  relations between big and small, powerful and less powerful. The protection of the weaker should be of para-
  mount importance.

The principle of reconciliation Since it is entirely normal
  for there to be inequalities and anomalies in such a
  complex mosaic of countries, economies, cultures and
  democracies, a *policy of reconciliation* is needed between
  stronger and weaker partners. Disagreements ought not
  to be exacerbated by put-downs and accusations.

The principle of non-exploitation Finally, safety mechanisms must be built into the political architecture of
  Europe to prevent the powerful countries from exploit-
  ing the weaker partners for their own profit.

A German Europe violates these basic principles of any
viable European society. Tactics such as delaying decisions and taming and disciplining weaker members
destroy the mutual trust of ordinary citizens. They turn
the vision of a united Europe into its opposite: the vision
of Europe as an enemy.

3
A Social Contract
for Europe

Are we en route to a post-European era, a paradoxical revival of a continent of small states in the age of globalization? Have the perceptions of threat and insecurity become so great that we become attracted to the old clarity and seek refuge in a nineteenth-century future? Or does the shock we feel when we realize that the European Union may be facing its own destruction signal the beginning of a historic turning point from a European politics and society dominated by nation-states to a new transnationalism?

Let us imagine for a moment that we could construct the most amazing, most beautiful and most wonderful Europe which our minds are able to conceive – of what use would that be if ordinary citizens did not want it? What would Europe have to look like for ordinary people to think of it not as a nightmare but as their heart's dearest desire? A Europe whose demise would make us feel as if a small part of ourselves had died? A Europe worth living for and fighting for and that we would gladly vote for?

The possible disintegration of Europe has been scrutinized from the point of view of its political institutions, its economy, its elites, its governments and its legal system, but not from the standpoint of the individuals who inhabit it. But what does Europe mean for individual human beings and what principles may be inferred from that for a new social contract for Europe? That is the question I should like to discuss in this final section. I shall attempt to supplement (and also break with) the usual institutional view of the EU by taking account of the individual's point of view. I shall not focus here on building a sort of Lego set of European institutions (Fiscal Compact, eurobonds, banking union, etc.). My interest is not so much in abstract institutional structures as in their implications for individuals and what they mean for them. This is linked to the question of the meaning of 'a European society of individuals'.

To what extent do ordinary citizens – i.e., the actual holders of sovereign power – support the political expansion of Europe? Do these individuals realize in their heart of hearts that, if Europe is to free itself from its current mess, it will have to create new institutions? And that such institutions can be created only with a great joint effort, by means of cross-border cooperation? Is not the willingness to give up on Europe without much thought based on the unbroken certitude that Europe exists, a certitude that makes it impossible to imagine what it would be like if suddenly there were to be no Europe? And now, when the risk is at its greatest, is not people's willingness to put their heart and soul into the European project ultimately much greater than the doubters would have us believe, and more genuine than the nostalgia for the nation-state that has been so overblown in the media? And could we not recruit this goodwill to feed into policies that envisage something very different from Merkiavelli's vision of a German Europe?

One possible approach might be found in Jean-Jacques Rousseau, specifically in his *Contrat Social* (1762), a text that continues to fascinate the modern reader. Rousseau showed that, when people wish to overcome the state of nature (*l'état de nature*), they are able to discover a way to freedom and identity in the community by means of a social contract. Today, at the beginning of the twenty-first century, we face the task of overcoming nationalism and finding our way to a European social contract. In what follows I would like to take up Rousseau's ideas and show what should be inscribed in such a contract and how it could be put into practice.

More freedom through more Europe

Europe is not itself a one-nation society, nor can it become one, since it is composed of a number of national democracies. And, from the point of view of the nation-state, Europe is not a society either. European 'society' should rather be thought of as a post-national society consisting of nation-states. The challenge this poses is to find a form of European community that deploys its communal power to provide legal protection to every individual in each nation and, at the same time, enriches each individual who associates with individuals who speak other languages and come from other political cultures, and makes them freer than before.

The French sociologist Vincenzo Cicchelli has researched Europe's younger generation in his latest book, *L'Esprit cosmopolite: voyages de formation des jeunes en Europe*.[1] His study makes it clear why Europe, understood as a space in which social experience is available, means an increase in freedom and cultural capital:

> Everywhere in Europe young people realize that the culture of their native country is undoubtedly important and a determining factor in their identity, but that it does not suffice for an understanding of the world. Young people must get to know other cultures since they sense that cultural, political and economic questions are closely tied up with globalization. This means that they must rub up against otherness, against cultural pluralism. This is a lengthy learning process involving travel for tourism, humanitarian and study purposes but even at home one should interest oneself in the cultural products of others – cinema, TV series, novels, cookery and fashion.[2]

In this way the young generation experiences European society as a 'twofold sovereignty', as the sum of national and European opportunities for development. Young people do not describe their identity as exclusively European, as is often expected. No one is simply and solely a European. Young people define themselves as nationals of a particular country *in the first instance* and *then* as Europeans. A Europe without frontiers and with a common currency offers them a hitherto unprecedented mobility, and it does so in a space with an enormous cultural wealth and a large number of languages, histories, museums, cuisines, etc.[3]

Cicchelli's study also shows, however, that, under the impact of the present crisis, this experience of Europe has started to crumble. The return of old rivalries and prejudices (for example, between the southern and northern countries) tends increasingly to undermine mutual recognition. What is even more striking is that the younger generation regards the world of Brussels institutions as remote, abstract and opaque. The young have the European experience – but without Brussels. Daniel Brössler writes about this in the *Süddeutsche Zeitung*:

> The problem is not the absence of a European sentiment but the fact that there are at least two different ones. There is the positive feeling of the great majority who would not like to miss out on any of the great European freedoms. And there is also the uneasy feeling, often in the same people, that a parallel universe exists far away in Brussels that has nothing in common with one's own life.[4]

For all the ambivalence it may still be asserted that more and more people, young ones especially, are living a European life. We need think only of the countless Erasmus students in Madrid, Berlin or Kraków.

Is it not deeply puzzling that this experience of a lived Europe hardly ever receives a mention in the current debates about the crisis in Europe and the euro? In my view, this arises from the fact that politicians, but also political scientists specializing in Europe, think of Europe for the most part in *one-dimensional, institution-centred* terms. The process by which Europe is to grow together is seen as operating purely in a *vertical* direction. European institutions (whether the Commission or the Council) make a proposal that has then to be implemented by the national societies. Thus *vertical* Europeanization refers to the integration of the member states on an institutional plane.[5] As Cicchelli's study shows, this institutional aspect remains alien and opaque – while the Erasmus generation experiences Europe across all borders so that here integration may be said to be taking place on the *horizontal* plane. Thus the European society of living individuals escapes notice because it does not figure in the vertical integration with its focus on institutions, while conversely that vertical integration fails to register in the lived experience of individuals. In short, on the one hand we have the abstract house of European institutions while the rooms in that house remain empty. On the other hand, there are the (young) individuals who live a European life but are reluctant to enter the house that is being built for them in Brussels. The crazy thing about this situation is that no one has noticed the contradiction.

During the past 150 years we have become accustomed to thinking of society in terms of the nation-state – i.e., as bound to a particular territory with clearly defined geographical frontiers, a judicial system valid for all citizens, a relatively homogeneous culture, a universal education system, an official language, and so forth. Young people in Europe today who have no problem with moving horizontally across borders, between Lisbon and Helsinki, Dublin and Thessaloniki, have a completely different view of European society. They experience Europe above all as a mobile society of individuals; they value the porousness of national frontiers, the multiplicity of cultures, languages, judicial systems, ways of life, etc. In this sense we can say that there is more freedom through more Europe.

More social security through more Europe

The new social contract must protect this great cosmopolitan freedom from meddling by orthodox adherents of the nation-state who yearn for a new clarity and new frontiers. But defending the present situation is not enough. The European society of individuals is threatened by a risk capitalism that corrodes moral milieus, allegiances and security, creates new risks and unloads them on the shoulders of individuals. The austerity policies with which Europe is currently responding to the financial crises unleashed by the banks are perceived as monstrous acts of injustice by ordinary citizens. After all, they have to pay in the hard currency of their material existences for the fecklessness with which the bankers simply gambled away quite unimaginable sums of money. It is actually high time to turn the tables on them. We do not need bailouts for the banks but rather a social lifeboat for the Europe of individuals. Such a Europe, characterized by its solidarity (one is tempted to resurrect the older term 'community'), would be fairer and more credible in the eyes of individuals. Hitherto, a lived freedom and the maximization of individual risks went hand in hand. If people are to experience Europe as something meaningful, the appropriate slogan must be 'More social security through more Europe!'

In the early 1980s, Ralf Dahrendorf predicted the end of 'the age of social democracy'.[6] This may be true on the national level. It is in fact the case that the vision of a social and environmental democracy has fallen into the sleep of the Sleeping Beauty with its well-established welfare state routines that fail to get to grips with the destructive force of global capitalism. People find themselves left to the mercies of the new risks; the typhoon of the credit crisis and the euro crisis has swept over the continent and dramatically intensified social inequalities in every society. The social question has now become the global question for which national solutions have ceased to exist. This amounts or comes close to a pre-revolutionary situation, to use an old-fashioned phrase. The anticipation of a catastrophe unleashes its own mobilizing force here too.

The new social contract that aims to win over individuals to Europe must attempt to initiate a social-democratic era on a transnational plane. In so doing, it must determine how to design a utopian but realistic system of social security that will not be doomed to end up in either of the two blind alleys: in the nostalgia for the national welfare state or in the reformist zeal of neo-liberal self-surrender. How are we to awaken Europe's and the world's social and environmental conscience and turn it into a political protest movement? How can the furious Greeks, unemployed Spaniards, worried Germans – in other words, the members of the individualized middle classes who are now staring into the abyss – be induced to come together as a Europe-wide or even worldwide political entity that will enforce the adoption of the new social contract?

To achieve this, the established political parties would have to succeed in something akin to squaring the circle. Their organizations and programmes will have to be adapted to fit the transnationalism of European politics while simultaneously winning national elections.

More democracy through more Europe

Change in Europe is frequently considered from the standpoint of institutions. If we ask questions about more democracy, this simply produces proposals for institutional reforms. We then find ourselves embroiled in discussions of the powers of the European Parliament, etc., but we also have to pose the question of democracy from the perspective of individuals, *from below*, so to speak, from the teeming mass of individuals who constitute horizontal integration. Only when people are able to regard Europe as their own project and learn how to adopt the perspective of the citizens of other European countries will it become at all meaningful to talk about vertical integration and European democracy.

So it is mutual understanding that is at issue here, the ability to see the world as others see it and to develop the cosmopolitan gaze. What that looks like can be seen from the following quotations. Birgit Schönau, the Italian correspondent for the *Süddeutsche Zeitung* and *Die Zeit*, writes from the perspective of the southern nations and describes their view of the policies of the German government and the international institutions:

> Save, save, save. Inform. Slim down, crank up the economy. And, if you don't mind, do it all at the double. Otherwise, sit down, that's a fail. The south's schoolmistresses are two in number; at first sight they are very different from each other. There is the elegant Frenchwoman Christine Lagarde and the resolute German Angela Merkel. With Lagarde there is never a hair out of place; she cultivates an ascetic appearance; on principle she never even allows herself a

glass of wine. Merkel is not quite so strict with herself and her hair. But she is perfectly strict with other people.[7]

This vision of these two powerful women bears the stamp of Protestant asceticism: 'They know nothing of absolution, of forgiveness.' 'They themselves would of course deny this, but the south feels that is how it is.' 'The south feels that is how it is.' These words signal the introduction of a cosmopolitan change of view. 'The north' comes to see itself differently in the gaze of 'the south'.

Writers who are sceptical about the possibility of building a European society frequently argue that nation-states are integrated on the basis of shared values. Such values are not to be found at present at the European level. Instead there are numerous conflicts, disagreements about rescuing the euro and the austerity policies. Birgit Schönau even speaks of a 'culture war' [*Kulturkampf*]. In this conflict-ridden Europe the cosmopolitan gaze could bring people together. This would mean, for example, that individual Germans would learn how to put themselves in the position of Greeks and 'see' what frightens, torments, embitters and infuriates them, and not least how Germany's actions appear to them and why they interpret them as arrogance, ignorance and a new imperialism. And it also means that individual Greeks would place themselves in the position of Germans and 'see' why many Germans accuse the Greeks of corruption, profligacy and a lax attitude towards paying their taxes.

If the ability to see the other person's point of view is the prerequisite for the emergence of a European democracy, we need a campaign to instil into Europeans the basic elements of cosmopolitan literacy. How are we to go about overcoming the cultural hegemony of the Eurosceptics, who acknowledge only an anaemic Sunday version of Europe, and create instead an everyday Europe of ordinary citizens? How can we ensure that as many individuals as possible have the opportunity to see themselves through the eyes of others? How can we make common cause with others the foundation of democratic participation in Europe?

'Doing Europe' – that was the answer given by Helmut Schmidt, Jürgen Habermas, Herta Müller, Senta Berger, Jacques Delors, Richard von Weizsäcker, Imre Kertész and other prominent Europeans in May 2012. Because they believe that European democracy has to grow *from the bottom up*, because they have grasped the fact that there is no 'European nation' but only a Europe of individuals who have still to become the sovereigns of European democracy, they have championed the introduction of a voluntary European year for all.[8] In future everyone should have the opportunity to see something of Europe from below, in another country, where a different language is spoken – not just the younger generation and members of the educational elite, but ordinary working people, pensioners and the unemployed.

Let us assume for a moment that this voluntary European year for all were already a reality. Frank Schuster, forty-four, a bank employee in Lüneburg, has worked for a year on an environmental project in Athens and made new friends during this period. He has seen how the mother of a Greek friend had her pension reduced several times, how neighbours had to move out because they could no longer pay the rent, how shops had to shut down in the street where he was living, and how deeply humiliated people felt as a consequence of the austerity policies. Having returned to Germany, he was astounded to see the 'bankrupt' Greeks being torn apart in the media, politics and everyday conversations. Whereas in Germany the Greeks are generally accused of living above their means, he has seen the very opposite. More and more people in Greece are being plunged into poverty.

Or take Brigitte Reimann from Passau. She is a 28-year-old media designer who was initially unable to find a job after graduation but is now working in Warsaw on a project to produce a German-Polish history textbook. Her reception was very friendly but there were times when she found that the German-imposed austerity programme awakened memories of Germany's militant imperialism. On one occasion a pensioner living nearby burst out furiously with the question: 'What did your grandfather actually do during the war?' She gave him a look and replied, 'My grandfather was fourteen years old when the war ended.' Her neighbour was momentarily taken aback and then said quietly, 'I beg your pardon.'

The voluntary European year would institutionalize what Charles Taylor has referred to as the 'dance of understanding', and it suggests an answer to the question of what Europe means to Europeans. It would make democratic identification and participation possible for individuals and in that way establish an often critical connection between their own life and actions and what many people think of as the technological Nirvana that goes by the name of Brussels.

Whoever equates the deficits of European democracy with the issue of the relationship between national parliaments and the European Parliament or between national constitutional courts and the European Court of Justice can easily overlook the fact that here too democracy is being thought of in vertical terms. What is excluded is how the citizens of each nation can become sovereign Europeans. The ideal by which the realization of European democracy is frequently measured today has its roots in the era of nation-states. That era had 'peoples' whose will was represented and translated into action by democratic institutions. This does not happen in the Europe of individuals. It follows that democracy can come alive only to the degree that people take possession of the project and build Europe together. That is precisely what is meant by 'more democracy by Doing Europe'.

The perspective of a Europe from the bottom up remains incomplete unless we round it off it by taking a look at the architecture of the institutions of a European democracy. Among other dilemmas to be resolved is the question of how to preserve national democracy at a time when transnational democracy is gaining in authority. From the standpoint of individuals, the defect of the previous architecture lies in the fact that elections to the European Parliament do not really result in decisions about the destiny of Europe. And even if such elections really did enable voters to take decisions on matters affecting Europe, there would still be a lack of clarity about the financial resources with which to implement those decisions. After all, Europe is dependent on funds flowing from the member states – a fact highlighted by the debt crisis. This means that a democratic Europe really needs its own pot of money. We can of course easily imagine the reaction of Europe's citizens to the idea that they should give up a part of their income in order to fund 'European solidarity' or if VAT were raised and the additional income were passed on to the Commission. This is the point at which we might consider the much discussed financial transaction tax, a bank tax or an EU-wide profits tax. This would be used, on the one hand, to help mitigate the worst excesses of a risk capitalism out of control while, on the other hand, it would finally enable a democratic Europe to initiate actions of its own.

This may well sound hopelessly utopian and naïve. But if Europe and the euro are really threatened with breakdown we surely have to think again. Indeed the present crisis must lead to a rethinking of realism. What has been considered 'realistic' up to now has become naïve and dangerous because it acquiesces in that break-down. And what has up to now been regarded as naïve and delusional becomes 'realistic' because it attempts to forestall disaster and incidentally to make the world a better place.

The question of power: who will enforce the social contract?

Whoever inquires how a new social contract might be introduced and become effective in Europe must go in search of an alliance of cosmopolitan countries that are able and willing to assume a vanguard role in order to restore their national position and dignity in Europe and the world. Which countries would come into considera-tion for the construction of such a cosmopolitan coalition?

In terms of power relations, this coalition would have to be forged between countries at present labouring under a great burden of debt (which they are unable to dismantle on their own and for which they require European cooperation and solidarity) and countries that have profited from Europe hitherto and whose profits are now threatened by the possible collapse of the euro or even the EU. The first category includes Italy and Spain, and perhaps France as well in the not too distant future. The France of François Hollande would first have to come to terms with the fact that it is no longer *la Grande Nation*, though here too there is a Machiavellian subtext: the more France comes under pressure economically, the more attractive is the prospect of celebrating its resurrection in a political European Union.

At the present time the second category comprises Germany first and foremost. Germany has undoubtedly profited politically, morally and economically from Europe, from the euro and also from the crisis. Pressing for European political union is therefore very much in its interest. Paradoxically, those who nowadays advocate going it alone are really acting unpatriotically because they fail to recognize that it would amount to political suicide if Europe were to come to grief because of German stinginess, for without Europe and the euro Germany's own welfare state could not be defended.

Thus, in contrast to the widespread pessimism, we can say that, looked at 'realistically', all the above countries (and why shouldn't states such as Poland also be included?) have an interest in greater cooperation and European solidarity and hence in the introduction of a new social contract for Europe.

Let us assume that such a change in national mood were to take place in Germany (and a change in power might also be necessary), and the country were to put itself at the head of this coalition. What levers of power would be needed to establish the new social contract as a practical reality? The Merkiavellian power calculus would have to be modified in principle. Whereas hitherto the granting of credits has been tied to budgetary discipline and neo-liberal reforms, in the future it would have to be tied to the readiness to support the new social contract, to cede various sovereign powers such as control of one's own budget for the sake of European autonomy and in this way, step by step, to create a political union. As Jan Hildebrand writes in *Die Welt*, 'Whoever wants debts to be incurred jointly would have to accept that from now on income and expenditure could no longer be decided on separately.'[9]

The key point here is that the levers of power would have to be so designed that both things – the joint-liability union and the social contract – would have to come into existence at the same time. For example, at the moment, François Hollande, the new French president, wants to make a start with joint liability right away and introduce a new political union at a later stage, although this might well mean waiting for pigs to fly. But, with an impending catastrophe on the horizon, it would surely be advisable to introduce the two things simultaneously. If that could be done successfully, it might even be possible to win over two further allies for a European social contract: first – and this may seem to be a paradox – the players in the global financial markets who, in the event of a clear commitment to a political Europe, might well feel more confident and able to invest, since it would be clear that, in the event of a new crisis, there would be an authority that would assume liability for any possible losses; and, second, the populations of the debtor nations who have been protesting against the neo-liberal austerity measures, but who might well identify with the project of a political Europe because it holds out the prospect of a transnational, social-democratic model.

A European spring?

As we have seen, from the standpoint of the sociological observer it would be in the interest of the member states referred to above to inscribe the introduction of a new European social contract on their banners. Moreover, it is a central proposition of the theory of risk that the anticipation of a catastrophe can lead people to do things tomorrow that were absolutely inconceivable yesterday. Nevertheless, it must be confessed that there is little to suggest that, at the moment, the German government or other governments might soon join the camp of the Europe builders. On this point I share Jürgen Habermas's scepticism: 'The rediscovery of the German nation-state, the new mode of short-term politics without a compass, and the coalescing of politics and the media into a single class may explain why politics lacks the stamina for such a major project as European unification.'[10] Does this mean that the prospects for a European social contract are somewhat passé for the moment? Not necessarily. Habermas writes:

> But looking upwards at the political elites and the media may be to look in completely the wrong direction. Perhaps the motivations which are currently lacking can only come from below, from within civil society itself. The phase-out of atomic energy is an example of the fact that the things

which are taken for granted in politics and culture, and hence the parameters of public discussion, do not change without the dogged, subterranean work of social movements.[11]

It is just eighteenth months since we witnessed an Arab spring which took everyone by surprise. The Arab spring was followed by a hot American autumn, when the activists of Occupy Wall Street occupied Zuccotti Park in New York. In a country where previously almost no one had doubted that capitalism was the best of all possible social systems, calls for alternatives suddenly made themselves heard. Occupy Wall Street claimed that it spoke for the 99 per cent of Americans who had been overwhelmed by the crisis as against the 1 per cent who had profited from it. And the cry 'We are the 99 per cent' reached young people not only in other American cities but also in London and Vancouver, Brussels and Rome, Frankfurt and Tokyo. The demonstrations were aimed suddenly not just against a single bad law or in favour of one particular measure but against 'the system' itself. What used to be known as the 'free market economy' and is now called 'capitalism' once again was put under the microscope and subjected to fundamental criticism – and for a moment the whole world listened. After the Arab spring and the American autumn, might there soon be a European autumn, winter or spring? Or resistance to the Euro-German austerity policy? Or a European social movement that is prepared to go onto the streets for the new social contract? Of course, in the last two or three years we have seen how young people in Madrid, Tottenham or Athens have protested about the effects of neo-liberal austerity policies and have drawn attention to their fate as members of a lost generation. Admittedly, we should note that even these demonstrations were in a sense still indebted to the dogma of the nation-state. People defend themselves in their individual countries against the German-European policy that is being implemented by their governments.

But it is high time for the cosmopolitan imperative to be taken to heart even by what Zygmunt Bauman calls the 'superfluous populations', the 'precariat' – i.e., the sections of the middle class threatened by the crash, well-qualified young people who have no prospects of permanent employment, old people whose pensions have been cut – in short, all the people Europe-wide who have been hit hard by the austerity policies and are regarded as 'collateral damage'. They must learn to cooperate across the frontiers and join forces to fight not for less Europe but for a political union *from below* that is committed to social-democratic principles, since only these would be in a position to combat the causes of their plight effectively.

Established politics and political science have one weakness in common. They chronically underestimate the power of the powerless, the power of social movements, especially in transnational risk conflicts. In order to understand these it makes sense to distinguish between institutionalized politics (parties, governments and parliaments) and the non-institutionalized sub-politics of social movements. The fact is that in recent decades it is the sub-political actors and networks not tied to national territories and priorities who have raised the issues of ecological survival, gender equality, peace and, not least, the financial crisis and put these on the agenda in the teeth of resistance from political, economic, scientific and media elites. In this sense, the mobilizing force of risk uncouples politics from the actors and forums that are supposed to preside over such matters. The cosmopolitan imperative 'Cooperate or be doomed' is especially suited to empowering social movements for Europe.

What has made it possible for such a Europe-wide movement to arise from below with such force? As we have seen, the euro crisis has definitively stripped neo-liberal Europe of its legitimacy. In consequence, there is an asymmetry between power and legitimacy. Great power and minimal legitimacy are to be found on the side of capital and of nation-states, minimal power and great legitimacy on the side of the protesters. The movement could take advantage of this imbalance to promote core demands in the teeth of the resistance of the narrow-minded, orthodox defenders of the nation-state and on behalf of Europe. One such demand would be for a European financial transaction tax, which, properly understood, is actually in the best interests of the states themselves. And who knows? This might lead to a coalition between the protest movement and vanguard of the Europe builders that would achieve the quantum leap into the ability to act transnationally.

As a challenge to the rush to the judgement that all action is hopeless, perhaps we can end with this insight. The most powerful opponents of the global finance industry are not the people who have erected their tents worldwide in the great squares and in front of the banks, those cathedrals of finance. The most convincing and most pertinacious opponent of the global finance industry is ultimately the global finance industry itself.

All this may remind us of Hölderlin's verse, of his consoling promise: 'But where danger lurks, the saving powers also grow.' Brought up to date and applied to Europe, we would have to say, where danger lurks, the lifeboats are at hand – and, at the same time, the opportunities for a powerful pro-European movement. As we can observe at present, the opposite is no less valid: with the lifeboats the danger grows too. For what we see arising from the euro crisis, irresistibly hitherto, is a German Europe.

Notes

Preface

1 Timothy Garton Ash, 'Angela Merkel needs all the help she can get', *The Guardian* (8 February 2012); available at www.guardian.co.uk/commentisfree/2012/feb/08/angela-merkel-all-help-can-get?INTCMP=SRCH (accessed September 2012).

Introduction

1 'Akropolis Adieu!' This was the title of an article in *Der Spiegel* (14 May 2012).
2 See 'Griechische Spargegner führen in Umfrage zur Wahl', *Zeit online* (25 May 2012), www.zeit.de/politik/ausland/2012-05/griechenland-wahl-syriza (accessed August 2012).
3 One could use the English word 'leadership' even in German, whereas the German word 'Führung' is still contaminated by its association with Hitler, *Der Führer*, and the National Socialists.
4 Birgit Schönau, 'Das wäre die vierte Schuld', interview with Eugenio Scalfari, *Die Zeit* (15 March 2012), 7.

Chapter 1 How the Euro Crisis is both Tearing Europe Apart and Uniting It

1 For these figures, see Eurostat, 'Jugendarbeitslosenquote in den Mitgliedsstaaten der Europäischen Union im Juni 2012 (saisonbereinigt)', available at http://de.statista.com/ statistik/daten/studie/74795/umfrage/jugendarbeitslosig-keit-in-europa/ (accessed August 2012); Wirtschaftskammer Österreich, 'Jugendarbeitslosenquote 2001–2011', available at http://wko.at/statistik/Extranet/bench/jarb. pdf (accessed August 2012); Veronica Frenzel, Albrecht Meier, Sigrid Kneist and Matthias Thibaut, 'Europas verlorene Jugend', *Der Tagesspiegel* (10 August 2012), available at www.tagesspiegel.de/politik/krawalle-ueberall-europas-verlorene-jugend/4486172.html (accessed August 2012).

2 Holger Gertz, 'Ich versteh kein Wort. Nie wurde soviel geredet – und nie standen die Menschen den Krisen dieser Welt so ratlos gegenüber. Eine Reise an die Börse, in die Politik, auf die Straße. Zu einem diffusem Phänomen: Angst 2.0', *Süddeutsche Zeitung* (27 August 2011), 3.

3 Ulrich Beck, *Risk Society: Towards a New Modernity* (London: Sage, 1992); Beck, *World Risk Society* (Cambridge: Polity, 1998).

4 In this sense, risk society is another term for a manufactured not-knowing; see on this point Ulrich Beck, 'Knowledge or unawareness? Two perspectives on reflexive modernization', in Beck, *World Risk Society* (Cambridge, and Malden, MA: Polity, 1999), 109–32; Ulrich Beck and Peter Wehling, 'The politics of non-knowing: an emerging area of social and political conflict in reflexive modernity', in *The Politics of Knowledge*, ed. Fernando Dominguez Rubio and Patrick Baert (London and New York: Routledge, 2012), 33–57.

5 Antonio Gramsci, 'Past and Present', in *Prison Notebooks*, ed. Joseph A. Buttigieg, trans. Joseph A. Buttigieg and Antonio Callari (New York: Columbia University Press, 1996), vol. II, §34, pp. 32–3.

6 The allusion here is to the transition from the first modernity to the second. See, on this point, Ulrich Beck, Wolfgang Bonss and Christoph Lau, 'The theory of reflexive modernization: problematic, hypotheses and research programme', *Theory, Culture & Society* 20/2 (2003), 1–33; Ulrich Beck and Christoph Lau, 'Second modernity as a research agenda: theoretical and empirical explorations in the meta-change of modern society', *British Journal of Sociology* 56/4 (2005), 525–57.

7 Wolfgang Streeck, 'Die Krisen des demokratischen Kapitalismus', *Lettre International*, 95 (2011), 7–13.

8 Wolfgang Münchau, 'The prize for European political illiteracy', *Financial Times* (8 April 2012); available at www.ft.com/intl/cms/s/0/48d37a50-7da4-11e1-bfa5-00144feab49a.htm#axzz22rtQ3XTq (accessed September 2012).

9 Ibid.

10 Ulrich Beck, *The Reinvention of Politics: Rethinking Modernity in the Global Social Order*, trans. Mark Ritter (Cambridge, and Malden, MA: Polity, 1999), 6f.; *Power in the Global Age: A New Global Political Economy*, trans. Kathleen Cross (Cambridge: Polity, 2005).

11 In their recent European initiative, the German Social Democrats Sigmar Gabriel and Peer Steinbrück have proposed the issuing of bonds with joint liability. We shall have to wait and see how far this represents a significant exception. Steinbrück is very well aware of the risks associated with this proposal. In an interview in the *Süddeutsche Zeitung* in August 2012, he said: 'We have no choice but to keep on explaining the position of Europe in a world that is subject to a hectic rate of change. I am thinking here not just of the economy but also in political, cultural and social terms. We have to keep reminding people that peace and prosperity cannot be taken for granted, but that we have to work away at a policy of integration.' (Susanne Höll and Claus Hulverscheidt, 'Das wird schwer für die SPD', interview with Peer Steinbrück, *Süddeutsche Zeitung*, 11 August 2012, 8).

12 Quoted in Helene Cooper, 'World leaders urge growth, not austerity', *New York Times* (19 May 2012), available at www.nytimes.com/2012/05/20/world/world-leaders-at-us-meeting-urge-growth-not-austerity.html? pagewanted=all (accessed September 2012).

13 Dirk Kurbjuweit, Ralf Neukirch, Christian Reiermann and Christoph Schult, 'Europa der zwei Europas', *Der Spiegel*, 44 (2011), 24–8; available at www.spiegel.de/spiegel/print/d-81302966.html (accessed July 2012).

14 Quoted in 'Schäuble: Die Löhne können kräftig steigen', *Frankfurter Allgemeine Zeitung* (5 May 2012); available at www.faz.net/aktuell/wirtschaft/tarifverhandlungen-schaeuble-die-loehne-koennen-kraeftig-steigen-11740624.html (accessed August 2012).

15 See Ulrich Greiner, 'Die Antike in Ehren', *Die Zeit* (31 May 2012).

16 Friedrich Nietzsche, 'Book Five: We fearless ones', in *The Gay Science*, ed. Bernard Williams, trans. Josefine Nauckhoff (Cambridge: Cambridge University Press 2001), 242 [translation slightly varied].

Chapter 2   Europe's New Power Coordinates: The Path to a German Europe

1 A distinction should be observed between *social change* and the *transformation* of the social and political order. Elsewhere I have drawn a distinction between social change and 'fundamental change' (in the sense of a change in the 'reference system of change' or 'metachange'). See Ulrich Beck, 'Beyond class and nation: reframing social inequalities in a globalizing world', *British Journal of Sociology* 58/4 (2007), 679–705.

2 The relevant authors go on to inquire with reference to the present and the future about how society continues to reproduce itself, whether in the class system (Pierre Bourdieu), the system of power (Michel Foucault), the bureaucracy (Max Weber) or the (autopoietic) system (Niklas Luhmann). Whereas these writers all have in mind

the normal workings of politics and society and demon-strate their ingenuity in exposing existing institutions' resistance to change, my theory of global risk focuses on the exceptional case that throws established routines into chaos. The fact is that this exceptional case has become the norm in the world risk society.

3 It is customary to speak of 'crisis', but I prefer here to speak of 'risk' for the most part. But how do these two concepts relate to each other? The term 'European risk' which I have introduced here contains the term 'Euro-crisis' (or 'European crisis') but goes beyond it in three respects. *First*, the concept of crisis blurs the distinction between the (staged) risk as the future-in-the-present and catastrophe as the present-in-the-future (of which we can ultimately know nothing). The talk of risk may be said to 'ontologize' the difference that is central here, between an anticipated catastrophe and an actual one. *Second*, the use of 'crisis' deceives us into imagining that by overcoming the crisis today we shall be able to revert to a pre-crisis state of affairs. In contrast, 'risk' exposes the 'secular dif-ference' between the impending global threat and the responses to it available to us in the framework of national policies. And that implies, *third*, that risk, in my under-standing of it, is – unlike crisis – not an exception but rather the normal state of affairs and hence will become the engine of a great transformation of society and politics.

4 This experience of possible catastrophe, namely the mor-tality of the euro, writes Lluís Bassets in the Spanish daily *El País*,

> is reminiscent of praying for rain. . . . The more often you repeat the prayer, the more vivid the bleak, unwel-come picture of a Europe without the euro and a world without Europe becomes. . . . We have all understood the situation perfectly. The euro is mortal; it may pass away in our arms in the next few days. . . . Mentally, we have already entered unknown terrain. . . . It is therefore hardly surprising that the European factories

producing papers, manifestoes, articles and emergency reports are using up their remaining hours in the search for a formula that would open the doors for eurobonds, for the solidarity that might bring salvation, for the transfer union that Germany has embargoed hitherto and that at the same time might guarantee the austerity policy, and the monitoring and responsible financial conduct that Angela Merkel has been calling for . . . the problem is that only a very few of these ideas are capable of being implemented quickly and that at a time when we have to place a bet on the markets about the mortality of the euro, their utility is far from proven. ('El euro es mortal', *El País* (28 June 2012); German translation available at www.presseurop.eu/de/content/press-review/2260291-ja-der-euro-ist-sterblich) (accessed August 2012).

5 See, for example, the writers referred to in note 2 above. For the most part politics is identified with national politics. What is meant, therefore, is that their *ideas* of national and international politics are at an end. The question of which new (transnational) forms of politics are emerging remains obscure. In the same way, Carl Schmitt based his thinking on the assumption of the dissolution of national politics. In the current crisis, however, what we have seen up to now has been the very antithesis of this. The member states of the EU are the key players in overcoming the European crisis.

6 Carl Schmitt, *Political Theology: Four Chapters on the Concept of Sovereignty*, trans. George Schwab (Cambridge, MA, and London: MIT Press, 1985), 15.

7 Ibid., 14.

8 Ibid., 13.

9 Severin Weiland, 'Der Traum vom neuen Europa', *Spiegel online* (12 June 2012), available at www.spiegel.de/politik/deutschland/eu-experten-suchen-in-bruessel-nach-weg-aus-der-euro-krise-a-838173.html (accessed August 2012).

10 Ibid.

11 Heribert Prantl, 'Wie lange noch? Die Europa-Politik der Kanzlerin missachtet und beleidigt das Bundesverfassungsgericht', *Süddeutsche Zeitung* (22 June 2012), 4.

12 Winfried Hassemer, 'Dalli, dalli, das Haus brennt!', *Frankfurter Allgemeine Zeitung* (28 June 2012), 33.

13 In 'Anatomie einer Hintergehung' [Anatomy of a sleight of hand], Christian Geyer takes issue with the style of government cultivated by Angela Merkel during the euro crisis, castigating the tendency towards de-democratization (in *Frankfurter Allgemeine Zeitung*, 21 June 2012, 29). Admittedly, he lays the blame for this exclusively at Angela Merkel's feet, evidently unwilling to acknowledge that political action under the spell of the threat to Europe finds itself caught in the structural dilemma of being both required by the situation and forbidden by law. Whether any further progress towards a *European* democracy will be endangered by the insistence on *national* democracy is a story that has still to be written.

14 Quoted from Wolfgang Proissl, 'Die EZB als Brunnenbauer der Euro-Zone', *Financial Times Deutschland* (12 June 2012), 24.

15 Udo Di Fabio, 'Ewige Bindung oder flüchtige Liaison?', *Frankfurter Allgemeine Zeitung* (6 October 2011); available at www.faz.net/aktuell/politik/staat-und-recht/der-westen-am-scheideweg-ewige-bindung-oder-fluechtige-liaison-11483302.htm (accessed August 2012).

16 Carl Schmitt, *The Concept of the Political*, trans., ed. and intro. George Schwab (New Brunswick, NJ: Rutgers University Press, 1976), 54.

17 See Severin Weiland, 'Der Traum vom neuen Europa'.

18 See Dirk Kurbjuweit, Ralf Neukirch, Christian Reiermann and Christoph Schult, 'Europa der zwei Europas', *Der Spiegel*, 44 (2011), 24–8; available at www.spiegel.de/spiegel/print/d-81302966.html (accessed July 2012).

19 Cerstin Gammelin, 'Endlich wieder sagen, was man will: Auf dem EU-Sondergipfel nehmen Europas Politiker mit unverhohlener Freude Abschied vom Duo Merkozy', *Süddeutsche Zeitung* (25 May 2012), 7.

20 Kurbjuweit et al., 'Europa der zwei Europas'.

21 Joschka Fischer, 'Vom Staatenverbund zur Föderation – Gedanken über die Finalität der europäischen Integration', speech given on 12 May 2000 at Humboldt University, Berlin; available at www.europa.clio-online. de/Portals/_Europa/documents/fska/Q_2005_FS7-09.pdf (accessed August 2012).

22 Damir Fras and Bettina Vestring, 'Kleineuropäische Vorstellungen funktionieren einfach nicht mehr', interview with Joschka Fischer, *Berliner Zeitung* (28 February 2004); available at www.berliner-zeitung.de/archiv/aussenminister-joschka-fischer-ueber-die-integration-der-tuerkei-den-ruecktritt-schroeders-als-spd-chef-und-eine-beziehung-zwischen-koch-und-keller-klein-europäische-vorstellungen-funktionieren-einfach-nicht-mehr,10810590,10155702.html (accessed August 2012).

23 The Romanian political scientist Alina Mungiu-Pippidi writes on this point:

> A friendly East-European diplomat complained with some bitterness recently that it was not exactly very polite on Europe's part to have fallen into crisis right after we had joined it. After a two-speed Europe had been resisted for years, it was with some perplexity that he saw this very idea lauded as the only viable solution. What is to be done? If we accept the kinds of solution put forward by Jean-Claude Piris [a lawyer involved in the elaboration of the Lisbon Treaty] – i.e., an additional treaty exclusively for those members of the eurozone who are in a position to make the transition to a financial federalism – that would put an end to the crisis of the euro, but it would mean that we have three Europes: an efficient, united eurozone, the lame-duck eurozone, which doesn't know whether it should try to advance or retreat (Greece, Portugal . . .), and those outside the eurozone who have no serious prospects of ever catching up with the others. ('Criza şi cele trei Europe', *România Liberă*, 14 November 2011; available in German trans. at www.presseurop.eu/de/content/

article/1169441-die-krise-und-dreierlei-europa [accessed August 2012])

24 According to Timothy Garton Ash ('Angela Merkel needs all the help she can get', *The Guardian*, 8 February 2012; available at www.guardian.co.uk/commentisfree/2012/feb/08/angela-merkel-all-help-can-get?INTCMP=SRCH):

> Yet because of the crisis of the eurozone this European Germany finds itself, unwillingly, at the centre of a German Europe. No one can seriously doubt that Germany is calling the shots in the eurozone. The reason we have a fiscal compact treaty agreed by 25 EU member states is that Berlin wanted it. Desperate, impoverished Greeks are being told to "do your homework" by Germans. . . . Germany did not seek this leadership position. Rather, this is a perfect illustration of the law of unintended consequences.

25 Eric Gujer, 'Die neue deutsche Frage', *Neue Zürcher Zeitung* (21 July 2012); available at www.nzz.ch/meinung/kommentare/die-neue-deutsche-frage-1.17383545 (accessed August 2012).

26 In *Cosmopolitan Europe* (trans. Ciaran Cronin, Cambridge, and Malden, MA: Polity, 2007), Edgar Grande and I have attempted a systematic analysis of this dual polity.

27 Kurbjuweit et al., 'Europa der zwei Europas'.

28 A similar form of power characterizes the relationship between the nation-states and mobile capital; see Ulrich Beck, *Power in the Global Age: A New Global Political Economy*, trans. Kathleen Cross (Cambridge: Polity, 2005), 52. The fact that this economic logic now also operates between states has become evident in the course of the financial crisis.

29 Niccolò Machiavelli, *The Prince*, trans. Luigi Ricci (New York: Mentor, 1952 [1935]), 98.

30 For Brendan O'Neill of the English online magazine *Spiked*, Merkel embodies the 'schizophrenic' love–hatred that characterizes many people's attitude towards the EU:

'EU power is seen as dangerous, but so is EU inaction; some see the EU as the wrecker of nations, others believe it isn't doing enough to rescue nations. The way Merkel and the EU are now treated reminds me of what Homer Simpson once said about beer – that it is "the cause of and the solution to all of life's problems".' See www.spiked-online.com/site/article/12511. (accessed August 2012).

31 In the Polish newspaper *Gazeta Wyborcza*, Piotr Buras points to the paradox that the European triumph of the German model of stability coincides with its historic failure:

> The monetary union is based on the German model; the European Central Bank was a copy of the Bundesbank. The failure of this 'Maastricht-Europe' effectively undermines two of the crucial assumptions of German policy. These are that the German solutions for Europe are the best solutions and that the German model of the economy thrives best in symbiosis with European integration. Both assumptions made sense before the onset of the crisis. Germany was supportive of an ever closer process of integration and acted as the driving force behind the establishment of the Common Market and the monetary union. All of this benefited Europe as a whole. . . . Today, this symbiosis is a thing of the past. . . . It is a paradox that Germany is being forced to reinvent itself at a time when its current model is more successful than ever: its economy is booming and its unemployment figures have never been lower. To change course at such a moment calls for a whole lot of courage and decisiveness, qualities that Frau Merkel evidently lacks. ('Koniec niemickiej Europy' [The end of German Europe], *Gazeta Wyborcza*, 14 June 2012; available in German trans. at www.presseurop.eu/de/content/article/2219711-das-ende-des-deutschen-europas [accessed August 2012]).

32 On this point, see Alexander Hagelüken, 'EZB in der Eurokrise: Draghi wagt den Drahtseilakt', *Süddeutsche Zeitung* (2 August 2012); available at www.sueddeutsche. de/wirtschaft/ezb-in-der-euro-krise-draghi-ein-drahtsei-lartist-mit-absturzgefahr-1.1430252 (accessed August 2012).

33 See also the discussion in Beck and Grande, *Cosmopolitan Europe*, pp. 84–6.

Chapter 3   A Social Contract for Europe

1 Vincenzo Cicchelli, *L'Esprit cosmopolite: voyages de formation des jeunes en Europe* (Paris: Presses de Sciences Po, 2012).

2 Isabelle Rey-Lefebvre, 'Die Pfade werden kurviger', interview with Vincenzo Cicchelli, *Süddeutsche Zeitung* (31 May 2012), 15.

3 In their manifesto *Für Europa* (Munich: Hanser, 2012, p. 64), Daniel Cohn-Bendit and Guy Verhofstadt write: 'To be a European is a surname, while your own nationality is your given name. Nationalities separate us, Europe is what unites us.'

4 Daniel Brössler, 'Das gefühlte Europa', *Süddeutsche Zeitung* (29 June 2012), 4.

5 Ulrich Beck and Edgar Grande, *Cosmopolitan Europe*, trans. Ciaran Cronin (Cambridge, and Malden, MA: Polity, 2007).

6 Ralf Dahrendorf, *Die Chancen der Krise: Über die Zukunft des Liberalismus* (Stuttgart: Deutsche Verlags Anstalt, 1983), 16ff.

7 Birgit Schönau, 'Der Süden', *Süddeutsche Zeitung* (16 June 2012).

8 Ulrich Beck and Daniel Cohn-Bendit, 'Wir sind Europa! Manifest zur Neugründung der EU von unten', *Die Zeit* (3 May 2012), 45. Anyone who wishes to support our appeal can do so online, at http://manifest-europa.eu/ allgemein/wir-sind-europa?lang=de (accessed August 2012).

9 Jan Hildebrand, 'Merkel hält Kurs', *Die Welt* (21 June 2012).

10 Jürgen Habermas, 'A pact for or against Europe?', in Habermas, *The Crisis of the European Union: A Response*, trans. Ciaran Cronin (Cambridge, and Malden, MA: Polity 2012), 127–39, here p. 137.

11 Ibid.